*drawing from wisdom's well*

# drawing from wisdom's well

stories,

celebrations,

and explorations

of courageous

women of faith

*Gloria Ulterino*

**ave maria press**   Notre Dame, Indiana

© 2002 by Ave Maria Press, Inc.

www.avemariapress.com

International Standard Book Number: 0-87793-954-3

Cover and text design by Katherine Robinson Coleman

Cover photo image of woman: Index Stock Imagery

Inside illustrations by Jane Pitz

Ocean image: www.comstock.com

Printed and bound in the United States of America.

*Library of Congress Cataloging-in-Publication Data*

Ulterino, Gloria.
   Drawing from wisdom's well : stories, celebrations, and explorations of courageous women of faith / Gloria Ulterino.
      p. cm.
  Includes bibliographical references.
  ISBN 0-87793-954-3 (pbk.)
  1. Worship programs. 2. Women in the Bible. 3. Women in Christianity. I. Title.
  BV199.W6 U48 2002
  264'.7--dc21

2002006557
CIP

To the women.

# Contents

• • • • • • • • • • • • • • • • • • • • • • • • • • • • • • • • • • • • • • •

## ACKNOWLEDGMENTS

In some sense, this book has been nearly a lifetime in the making. Certainly, it is the fruit of many life-giving and challenging experiences over the past twenty-two years. On this pilgrim path, I have encountered a number of people for whom I am profoundly grateful.

- The priests and lay ministers who lit the match of my "falling in love" with the liturgy of the Roman Catholic Church, and who led me to the study of theology over twenty years ago.

- Rev. Sebastian Falcone, my first scripture professor at St. Bernard's Institute, whose devotion to the Word of God ignited a similar passion within me.

- Rev. Dr. Melanie May, first Dean of the Women and Gender Studies Department of Colgate Rochester Divinity School, and all who helped me see the profound need for a more inclusive church on many levels.

- Prisca, Junia, and Phoebe, the subjects of my paper in the course "Women in the Pauline Literature," who took on human flesh for me. They so inspired me by their egalitarian ministry in Pauline communities at the very dawn of Christianity that I promised to "get the word out" on them.

- The Christian feminist scholars of the past twenty (or so) years, without whose passionate probing, questioning, and proposing of new approaches to both scripture and doctrine this book would never have been possible. I most appreciate their integrity, fidelity to the gospel, and respectful truth-telling, with an eye to lifting up not only women, but all of humanity, and creation itself.

- The sixteen scholars who authored and signed "The Madaleva Manifesto, A Message of Hope and Courage" on April 29, 2000 (Feast of Catherine of Siena) at Saint Mary's College in Notre Dame, Indiana. They invite us to "re-imagine what it means to be the whole body of Christ. The way things are now is not the design of God."

- The women in this book, and so many others, then and now, who continually help me to faithfully imagine.

- The women with whom I work in our storytelling ministry, "Women of the Well." They inspire me with their commitment to truth and passion for creative ways of telling the stories of faith-filled women. One of them, Judith Stellpflug, has read every single prayer service and essay of this book, lovingly encouraging me at every step along the way.

- Some dear friends and my family, who have stayed the course, stretching and supporting, nurturing and challenging me.

- Finally, there is one person without whom this book could never have become a reality. It has been a true joy to work with my editor, Bob Hamma. He has been an unfailing source of professional expertise, both as editor and author, of honest yet gentle criticism, and of genuine collaborative guidance throughout the entire process. I am truly blessed to be working with him.

In the end, as in the beginning, I am grateful to the God of us all . . . for nudges and unfailing inspiration . . . for challenges and unconditional love . . . and for any wisdom gleaned along the pilgrim path of life.

Once there was a woman with the courage to break into an all-male dinner party and anoint Jesus on the head. It was just before his Passion, and this was her way of letting him know that she understood and appreciated who he was. Jesus said in return, "Truly I tell you, wherever the good news is proclaimed in the whole world, what she has done will be told in remembrance of her."[1] But we have forgotten this woman and so many others. We have often dismissed them, distorted them, distorted their stories, and thought of them as unimportant.

And yet, something in the body of Christ longs for the full restoration of these magnificent women. Indeed, the penetrating work of contemporary feminist scripture scholars has begun to do just that, and this book provides yet more energy in that direction. It offers a unique blend of worship services, storytelling, and a brief information paper on each of the women highlighted in the services. These are prayer services in a woman's voice, but they are intended for the entire church. This book is one woman's attempt to give voice to a few of the many women who have been faithful to God throughout the years. This book is one woman's attempt to behold the treasury of their truth as part of the ongoing healing and restoring of Christ's body.

In one sense, this book began a little more than twenty years ago when I fell in love with the liturgy of the Roman Catholic church. Thus began my insistent, urgent, never-to-be-denied call to ministry in this church. In a more immediate sense, this book began in the spring of 1995, when I took a course titled "Women in Pauline Literature." At the time I wrote a paper on three women named in Romans 16:1-7: Prisca, Junia, and Phoebe. As I read and wrote, these women captured my imagination, my heart, and my mind, so much that I promised them I would "get the word out" on them. And I have done just that. My paper led to "Conversations With Women of the Early Church," a role play among these three women, with discussion. That led to the formation of a storytelling group, "Women of the Well," in January 1998, and now this book. Parish response to the storytelling presentations has been startling and fulfilling. People have said, "I have waited eighty years to hear the stories of women told in church! This is so powerful! It touches something in me that I didn't even know was there. We are thirsty for this!"

And this book is intended to quench thirst in many ways. The power of imagination, in a woman's voice, can forge a path through many a wilderness by raising consciousness, educating, and advocating for the full stature of women. The essays, faithful to post-Vatican II theology and scripture study, can offer new insights into women then and now. The prayer services can become a source of celebrations within and outside parish life. And these services, in conjunction with the essays, might be used for retreat/reflection times, for small Christian communities of every variety, for Bible study and R.C.I.A. groups, as well as for parish-wide educational opportunities. Those people who are gifted in storytelling might want to learn the parts and "become" the women. For those who are not gifted in this way, dramatic reading of the parts is also effective.

It is fitting that Prisca leads off this book, in worship and story. And it is fitting for me, personally, that Mary of Magdala concludes this book, for I have "become" Mary of Magdala on several occasions and continue to feel the power of her truth-telling. That is what this book is all about, and I have tried to do it with integrity, fidelity to scripture and tradition, creativity, and most of all, with the power of the Holy Spirit. My hope is that this book strikes a chord of truth in you, as well, and that you use it in a whole host of ways. In the end, my hope is that these services offer a way to praise God by celebrating, challenging, and healing God's people.

GLORIA ULTERINO
August 2001

Notes
1. See Mark 14:9.

# one

# PRISCA AND HER SISTERS IN MINISTRY

# We Are Called by Wisdom to Step Out in Faith

*Chairs are in a semi-circle, as if prepared for worship in a first-century house church. A table is prominent, left empty for the moment, until the entrance procession begins. There is a chair for Prisca at one side of the table, connecting her to the community.*

*Ministers:*    *Prisca, Junia, Phoebe, eight people in the entrance procession, cantor, and musicians*

*Materials:*    *large table, tablecloth, candles, scripture, a roll of paper to resemble a scroll, loaf of bread, small flask of wine*

## Introductory Rites

### WELCOME *(by Prisca)*

Welcome, everyone, to my house church in Rome! The year is 58, and it is early in the morning as we gather for our weekly worship on the first day of the week, the Lord's Day. Soon we will be off to work, as Sunday is a workday for us in the Roman Empire. But this time together will nourish us for the week ahead. My husband and coleader, Aquila, is out visiting someone who has taken ill. But we do have two guests, dear friends of mine, who also—like Aquila and me—know Paul well. Let me introduce them to you. Phoebe, the deacon and servant leader of the house church in Cenchreae, near Corinth, is here with a letter for us from Paul. And Junia, married to Andronicus and a relative of Paul's, was a member of the original Jerusalem community. She and her husband have preached the gospel with fervor and been in prison for the sake of the gospel, along with Paul. Now, please welcome them and introduce yourselves to one another, as we prepare for worship.

CALL TO WORSHIP                                    *Please stand*
· · · · · · · · · · · · · · · ·

All:        Listen!

Prisca:     "Does not Wisdom call,
            and does not understanding raise her voice?"

All:        Listen!

Prisca:     "On the heights, beside the way,
            at the crossroads she takes her stand."

All:        Listen!

Prisca:     "Take my instruction instead of silver,
            and knowledge rather than choice gold. . . ."
            "I am standing at the door, knocking;

All:        if you hear my voice and open the door,
            I will come in to you and eat with you
            and you with me." (Prv 8:1, 2, 10; Rv 3:20)

OPENING HYMN
· · · · · · · · · · · · ·

"Wisdom's Feast," text by Omer Westendorf and music by Jerry Brubaker, World Library Publications, © 1998.

*There is an entrance procession, as follows: Two people carry a tablecloth, tent fashion, with one preceding the other. They are followed by two people carrying lighted candles, two carrying the book of scripture and a scroll on which is written Romans 16:1-7, and a pair carrying a loaf of bread and a small flask of wine. When they arrive at the table, the two carrying the tablecloth go to either side of the table, lift up the cloth so that it billows, and then set it down on the table. They go in front of the table, facing the table, and wait. Each pair follows in turn, setting their items on the table and standing in front of the table; then all bow together before taking their seats.*

## OPENING PRAYER *(led by Prisca)*

. . . . . . . . . . . . . . . . . . . . . . . . . . .

Let us pray. . . .
O God of Wisdom,
lover of humanity,
dancer among the sun, moon, and stars,
you stand at our gates and call us by name,
pitching your tent, building your house in our midst.
Root us in your Wisdom, we pray,
that we might taste your honeyed goodness
and release your penetrating, searching, enduring love
in this time, in this place.
We make all this prayer in the name of Jesus,
your child and prophet.
Amen.

# Liturgy of the Word

. . . . . . . . . . . . . . . . . . . . . . . . . . . . . . . . . . . . . . . . . . . . .

## FIRST READING: PROVERBS 9:1, 2B, 3, 5-6 *(read by Junia)*

. . . . . . . . . . . . . . . . . . . . . . . . . . . . . . . . . . . . . . . . .

*Please be seated*

Wisdom has built her house,
she has hewn her seven pillars. . . .
She has mixed her wine,
she has also set her table.
She has sent out her servant-girls,
she calls from the highest places in the town. . . .
"Come, eat of my bread
and drink of the wine I have mixed.
Lay aside immaturity, and live,
and walk in the way of insight."

## PSALM 16

. . . . . . .

"You Will Show Me the Path of Life," refrain 1; text and music by
Marty Haugen, GIA Publications, Inc., © 1988.

## SECOND READING: ROMANS 16:1-7 *(read by Phoebe)*

I commend to you our sister Phoebe, a deacon of the church at Cenchreae, so that you may welcome her in the Lord as is fitting for the saints, and help her in whatever she may require from you, for she has been a benefactor of many and of myself as well.

Greet Prisca and Aquila, who work with me in Christ Jesus, and who risked their necks for my life, to whom not only I give thanks, but also all the churches of the Gentiles. Greet also the church in their house. Greet Mary, who has worked very hard among you. Greet Andronicus and Junia, my relatives who were in prison with me; they are prominent among the apostles, and they were in Christ before I was.

## HOMILY *(by Prisca)*

I've heard about you. For you are a generation marked by Wisdom. You know Jesus. You know that Jesus ate with everyone—saint and sinner, slave and free, woman and man, the "in group" and the outcasts, the rich and those with nothing, the sick and the healthy. You know that Jesus challenged everyone to live as God intends but that he never denied anyone a place at the table. With Jesus, there was always more than enough to go around . . . with some left over, besides. Like us who were there at the beginning, you want to open this feast to everyone.

Do you dream? And get discouraged? Or frustrated? And then, keep on going? Yes, so did we. Let me tell you how it was for us. It all began in the 40s in Rome . . . for that was when Aquila and I encountered Jesus for the first time! What passion we heard in his disciples! Oh, how they set our hearts on fire! And we, good Jews that we were, knew we had found the Promised One. It wasn't long before *our* passionate preaching attracted others, as well . . . and our first house church was born. What lighthearted, fulfilling days those were.

Then came our first great test of faith. By now, there was tension . . . Jewish brother against brother, sister against sister. There were those— like Aquila and me—who simply *knew* that Jesus was the Messiah, and others who just couldn't believe. Finally, Emperor Claudius had had enough . . . and sent us all packing. Where would we go? What would we do? Oh, how I prayed for Wisdom. How I *felt* like Wisdom, searching for a place to pitch my tent.[1] Aquila and I were tentmakers, you see. But, then, that was it! We would go to Corinth! For the Isthmian Games in honor of Poseidon were held every May and June just outside Corinth and people would need our services.

So, off we went. And wouldn't you know that God would have a surprise or two in store for us. For that was where we met Paul! And life would never be the same again.

He introduced us to Phoebe, who became like a soul sister to me. How we both loved to preach and pastor! And how we would laugh, trading stories about Paul. I told *her* about the time Paul urged us to go to Ephesus with him. And right away he got himself into trouble, preaching in the amphitheater dedicated to the goddess Artemis. Why, Demetrius the silversmith immediately started a riot, and we just barely got Paul out of harm's way *that* day. Then *she* told me about all the times he would get in trouble with the local officials, and the number of times she bailed him out with all her connections.

It was hard, at times, certainly. But we loved one another . . . deeply . . . and we treasured the path that God had put us on.

My friends, you are like us in so many ways. You never saw Jesus in the flesh either. But, just like us, you have heard his stories, and they burn within you. Yes, you ponder where to go and what to do next. And you try—as we did—to take the next right steps to build a church . . . one rooted in the Wisdom of Jesus, and to set the kind of table that Jesus would love to host. In our day, we wove a tapestry of tears and laughter, of hope imagined and dreams unfulfilled, of wisdom and failure. It was a tapestry marked with our life-blood, and it was all that we had to offer. We hand it on to you as a mantle. Pick it up! Let it become a symbol of Wisdom's feast. Let it become a challenge to bring our collective vision to life. Now is the time.

## Response to the Word

### RITUAL OF COMING TO THE TABLE (*led by Prisca*)

In his day, Jesus hosted many a Wisdom Feast, and he asked us who follow him to do the same. In my day, we did our best, knowing full well that "there is no longer Jew or Greek, there is no longer slave or free, there is no longer male and female; for all . . . are one in Christ Jesus."[2] But the Wisdom Feast of Jesus is not yet a reality. Indeed, from all that

I hear and understand, in my day we may well have experienced greater equality and partnership than you know today, especially among male and female. I therefore invite you to formulate a prayer for the table, that it may yet provide the inclusive meal—the Wisdom Feast—that Jesus envisioned. Then, when you are ready, please come forward to bless and reverence the table in whatever way is comfortable and silently pray your prayer as you wish.

MUSIC *(during the ritual)*

"Now in This Banquet," text and tune by Marty Haugen, GIA Publications, Inc., 1986. Advent refrain may be used in place of the usual refrain:

God of our journeys, daybreak to night, lead us to justice and light. Grant us compassion, strength for the day, wisdom to walk in your way.

## Closing Rites

BLESSING/SENDING *(led by Prisca, Junia, and Phoebe)*      *Please stand*

Prisca:      Loving Creator God,
            "With you is wisdom, she who knows your works
            and was present when you made the world;
            she understands what is pleasing in your sight
            and what is right according to your commandments.

Junia:      Send her forth from the holy heavens,
            and from the throne of your glory send her,
            that she may labor at [our] side,
            and that [we] may know what is pleasing to you.

Phoebe:      For she knows and understands all things,
            and she will guide [us] wisely in [our] actions
            and guard [us] with her glory." (Wisdom 9:9-11)
            Trusting in Your goodness, we pray in the name of Jesus,
            the Christ.
            Amen.

• • • • • • • • • • • •

"All Are Welcome," text by Marty Haugen, tune "Two Oaks," GIA Publications, Inc., 1994.

NOTES
• • • • •

1. See Sirach 24:7-8.

2. See Galatians 3:28; this was a baptismal profession of faith.

# Prisca, Phoebe, and Junia: Leaders in the Early Church

Prisca lived in a man's world. As a house church leader in three communities in the mid-first century, she knew about the world of patriarchy. According to Webster, this is a social system in which the father is supreme in family or clan, with wife and children legally dependent on him. And yet, she also knew a more egalitarian mode of relationship in ministry, for Prisca (also known as Priscilla in the Acts of the Apostles) and her husband Aquila led house churches together in Rome, Corinth, and Ephesus. Indeed, her name most often appears first, whenever the pair is named, highly unusual in the first century and even today. In Romans 16:1-7, Paul describes them as coworkers; he also praises Phoebe as "deacon" of the house church in Cenchreae (near Corinth), and Junia and Andronicus, another ministry pair, as "outstanding among the apostles."

Given that women of the first century are in the shadows, their voices a mere whisper at best, what can be said about them? The following information is gleaned—like seed for a renewed church—from studies by feminist scripture scholars like Elisabeth Schüssler Fiorenza, who make educated guesses based upon material available to us, from studies by scholars of the society of the day, and by the word studies of religious historians.

In her ground-breaking work, *In Memory of Her*, Elisabeth Schüssler Fiorenza imagines how it might have been in the first century. She notes that egalitarian modes of relationships were erupting in some religious circles, including many of the Pauline communities and some Jewish communities, as well, both of which attracted women. The Jesus movement, as she describes it, came out of a Jewish ethos dedicated to forging a "kingdom of priests and holy nation."[1] Within this context, Jesus offered a radical vision that would renew Judaism, a vision of inclusive wholeness. "Its central symbol is that of a festive meal to which everyone is invited, women as well as men, prostitutes as well as Pharisees."[2] While she agrees that our sources are skimpy, she points to Paul's window onto early church ministry in Romans 16:1-7; here "the practice of partnership/mission appears to have been the rule in the Christian missionary movement, which allowed for the equal participation of women with men in missionary work."[3] She maintains that Prisca, Junia, and Phoebe are among these women.

Those who study the first century world of the Roman Empire offer a picture that would support Fiorenza's assessment. Generally, patriarchy prevailed, as shown in the writings of the historian Tacitus. And yet, we have evidence of breakthroughs here and there. In the first century a gravestone acknowledged that one woman was connected with the theater.[4] At Pompeii, which provides a good sample of the economic activity open to women of the first century, free women could be found selling luxury items or exotic merchandise, like purple dye or perfumes, as well as working as butchers and fisherwomen. Women's names were also stamped on pipes and bricks, showing their participation in the building trades.[5] Amy Wordelman agrees with Fiorenza that "women also participated in private associations of many different sizes and shapes. . . . In a world that barred women from direct political power, these religious associations provided an arena in which women could and did exercise leadership roles."[6] Among these women, she says, were Prisca, Junia, and Phoebe.

Wayne Meeks fills out this picture in his significant work, *The First Urban Christians*. Beyond Palestine, he notes, Christianity was urban. Mobility among ministers was common, and it is estimated that Paul traveled ten thousand miles in his proclamation of the Gospel. Women shared in this mobility, he claims. In fact, he views them as upwardly mobile, no longer simply defined by the household where a relationship of dependence was the order of the day. A number of them worked with their hands and lived in commercial partnership with others.

Finally, in exploring the commercial connections of Phoebe, Caroline F. Whelan discovered that the legal documents of the day offered more freedom for women than might be supposed. There was the practice, for example, of "free marriage," quite common among the aristocracy by the second century, whereby "women were on an equal par with their husband in terms of ownership and disposal of property."[7] Women also had the right to make a will.

## A LETTER ARRIVES IN ROME

Early in the year 58, a letter arrived from Paul to Prisca and Aquila's house church in Rome. The letter concluded with Paul's recommendation of Phoebe, who was, most likely, the bearer of the letter.[8] Paul wrote his letter in Greek, but we read it now in English. Translations can make so much difference! They both reflect and affect what we know at any given time. In his 1980 *Commentary on Romans*, this is how scripture scholar Ernst Kasemann translated 16:1-7 (note my emphasis):

> I recommend to you Phoebe, our sister, a *deaconess* of the church at Cenchreae. *Receive her in the Lord as is fitting for the saints, and stand by her in any situation* in which she needs your aid. For she has been *a help* to many, and also to me personally. Greet Prisca and Aquila, my *fellow workers* in Christ Jesus, who risked their necks for my life, and to whom not only I, but all the churches of the Gentiles, owe thanks.
>
> Greet also the church in their house. Greet my beloved Epaenetus, the first born for Christ in Asia. Greet Mary, who has often toiled for you. Greet Andronicus and *Junias, my kinsmen* and (former) fellow prisoners, who are prominent among the Apostles and who were Christians before me.

Just a scant nine years later, the New Revised Standard Version would translate the emphasized words very differently . . . *because* of the work of people like Fiorenza and Wayne Meeks. Prisca and Aquila become "coworkers," Phoebe becomes a "deacon" and "benefactor" and Junia reclaims her womanhood! Let's take a closer look.

## WHO, THEN, IS PRISCA?

Prisca is clearly recognized in scripture as a significant leader of the church. She and Aquila had a house church in Ephesus (1 Cor 16:19), which means that their home was large enough to gather thirty to fifty people for worship on a weekly basis. She and Aquila taught the Alexandrian biblical scholar Apollos (Acts 18:26), and she and Aquila had a house church in Corinth (hinted at in Acts 18:26) and in Rome (Rom 16:3-5).

Prisca is "*sunergos*," one of Paul's coworkers, but not dependent on him. She and Aquila met Paul in Corinth, where they had a house church and went with Paul to Ephesus, where they also had a house church.

She is a Jewish Christian, very possibly a freed slave, and an artisan. She and Aquila are tentmakers. They probably were converted to Christianity in Rome but were forced to leave in the year 49 by a decree of Emperor Claudius.

## AND WHO IS PHOEBE?

Phoebe is "*diakonos*." Of the twelve times this word is used in the authentic Pauline letters, it refers to a man eleven times. In the King James Version, the translation is "minister" or "deacon" for the men, "servant" for Phoebe.[9] In the RSV translation, Phoebe is "deaconess," but many scholars now point out that this term is also incorrect; the term "deaconess" did not appear in church documents until late in the fourth century.[10] Fiorenza notes that "*diakonos*" is most often found in 2 Corinthians, where Paul refers to the "so-called pseudo-apostles who were charismatic missionaries, eloquent preachers, visionary prophets, and Spirit-filled apostles."[11] This must be true of Phoebe as well, she concludes.

Phoebe is "*prostatis*," often translated in the past as "helper," but scholars today paint a very different picture of that word. In the Hebrew scripture, "*prostatis*" is used for persons in authority.[12] Thus, "Paul, by calling Phoebe '*prostatis*' and '*diakonos*', was indicating that she deserved respect as an important church leader."[13] But there is more. The term, sometimes translated as "patron," has to do with the patron-client relationship in antiquity. As Fiorenza says, there is

> evidence that women joined clubs and became founders and
> patrons of socially mixed associations and cults. They

endowed them with funds for specific, defined purposes and expected honor and recognition in return for the benefactions. . . . Christians such as Phoebe acted as benefactors for individual Christians and the whole church. In dealings with the government or the courts they represented the whole community. With their network of connections, friendships with well-placed persons, and public influence, such benefactors eased the social life of other Christians in Greco-Roman society.[14]

Such relationships were complex. In the case of Paul and Phoebe, they would each share in the honor of the other's sphere of influence. One scholar even suggests that Paul sent Phoebe to Rome with this letter and instructions to gather support and resources for a future mission to Spain.[15]

In summary, Phoebe is a Gentile and a free woman who is not defined by her gender or marital status but by her ecclesial functions, very unusual in the first century. Finally, she is "our sister," similar to Timothy, "our brother."

### AND JUNIA?

She is a woman! And outstanding among the apostles! This is what John Chrysostom, who died in 407, had to say:

> "Greet Andronicus and Junia . . . who are outstanding among the apostles": to be an apostle is something great. But to be outstanding among the apostles—just think what a wonderful song of praise that is! They were outstanding on the basis of their works and virtuous actions. Indeed, how great the wisdom of this woman must have been that she was even deemed worthy of the title of apostle.[16]

Apparently, it was not until the commentator Aegidius of Rome (1245-1316) took the name to be masculine that she "became" a man! However, it was Martin Luther's lecture on the Romans that really set her name in concrete as masculine. In the original text, it appears in the accusative form with an "n" on the end. Is the masculine form with an "s" possible? Scholars today say no; the masculine name never existed, but Junia was a common name.

She is a Jewish Christian and very possibly a freed slave. Perhaps she and Andronicus were part of the original Jerusalem community. It is thought that Andronicus was a freed slave from Tarsus. They worked with Paul in Antioch and were in prison with him. They are true apostles, by Paul's definition, because they experienced the risen Christ and consciously accepted and endured the labors and sufferings associated with missionary work.

## WHY ARE THEY IMPORTANT?

These women assumed significant leadership roles in the earliest Pauline communities and they did so in equal partnership with men. It is obvious that Paul treasured their ministry and their very being. And they symbolize the baptismal creed that Paul proclaimed so eloquently in his letter to the Galatians (3:28): "There is no longer Jew or Greek, there is no longer slave or free, there is no longer male and female; for all of you are one in Christ Jesus." They symbolize a dream of an inclusive church today, with men and women in equal partnership.

## SOME RESOURCES

Arichea, Daniel C., Jr. "Who Was Phoebe? Translating Diakonos in Romans 16:1." *The Bible Translator* 39 (1988), pp. 401-409.

Bristow, John Temple. *What Paul Really Said About Women.* San Francisco: Harper, 1988.

Brooten, Bernadette J. "Early Christian Women and Their Cultural Context: Issues of Method in Historical Reconstruction." In *Feminist Perspectives on Biblical Scholarship.* Ed. Adela Yarbro Collins. Atlanta: Scholars Press, 1985, pp. 65-91.

_____. "Junia . . . Outstanding Among the Apostles (Romans 16:7)." In *Women Priests: A Catholic Commentary on the Vatican Declaration.* Ed. Leonard and Arlene Swidler. New York: Paulist Press, 1977, pp. 141-144.

_____. "Women and the Churches in Early Christianity." *Ecumenical Trends* 14 (1985), pp. 51-54.

Byrne, Brendan, S.J. *Paul and the Christian Woman.* Collegeville, MN: The Liturgical Press, 1988.

Castelli, Elizabeth A. "Romans." In *Searching the Scriptures.* Ed. Elisabeth Schüssler Fiorenza. New York: Crossroad, 1994, pp. 272-300.

Elliott, Neil. *Liberating Paul: The Justice of God and the Politics of the Apostle.* Maryknoll, NY: Orbis Books, 1994.

Fiorenza, Elisabeth Schüssler. *But She Said: Feminist Practices of Biblical Interpretation.* Boston: Beacon Press, 1992.

_____. "Missionaries, Apostles, Coworkers: Romans 16 and the Reconstruction of Women's Early Christian History." *Word and World* 6 (1986), pp. 420-433.

_____. "Remembering the Past in Creating the Future: Historical-Critical Scholarship and Feminist Biblical Interpretation." In *Feminist Perspectives on Biblical Scholarship*. Ed. Adela Yarbro Collins. Atlanta: Scholars Press, 1985, pp. 43-63.

Fitzmyer, Joseph A., S.J. "The Letter to the Romans." In *The New Jerome Biblical Commentary*. Ed. Raymond E. Brown, S.S., Joseph A. Fitzmyer, S.J., and Roland E. Murphy, O. Carm. Englewood Cliffs, NJ: Prentice Hall, 1990, pp. 830-868.

Gaventa, Beverly Roberts. "Romans." In *The Women's Bible Commentary, Expanded Edition*. Ed. Carol A. Newsom and Sharon H. Ringe. Louisville: Westminster John Knox Press, 1998, pp. 403-410.

Gerberding, Keith A. "Women Who Toil in Ministry, Even As Paul." *Current Trends in Theology and Mission* 18 (1991), pp. 285-291.

Jewett, Robert. "Paul, Phoebe, and the Spanish Mission." In *The Social World of Formative Christianity and Judaism: Essays in Tribute to Howard Clark Kee*. Ed. Jacob Neusner, Ernest S. Frerich, Peder Borgen, and Richard Horsley. Philadelphia: Fortress Press, 1988, pp. 142-161.

Kasemann, Ernst. *Commentary on Romans*. Grand Rapids, MI: William B. Eerdmans Publishing Company, 1980.

Lefkowitz, Mary R. and Maureen B. Fant. *Women's Life in Greece and Rome*. London: Gerald Duckworth and Co., 1982.

Meeks, Wayne. *The First Urban Christians*. New Haven: Yale University Press, 1983.

Moxnes, Halvor. "Honor, Shame, and the Outside World in Paul's Letter to the Romans." In *The Social World of Formative Christianity and Judaism*, as noted above, pp. 207-218.

Murphy-O'Connor, Jerome. "Prisca and Aquila: Traveling Tent Makers and Church Builders." *Bible Review* 8 (1992), pp. 40-51, 62.

Patterson, Lloyd G. "Women in the Early Church: A Problem of Perspective." In *Toward a New Theology of Ordination*. Ed. Marianne H. Micks and Charles P. Price. Somerville, MA: Greeno, Hadden, & Co., Ltd., 1976, pp. 23-41.

Petersen, Norman R. "On the Ending(s) to Paul's Letter to Rome." In *The Future of Early Christianity: Essays in Honor of Helmut Koester*. Ed. Birgir A. Pearson. Minneapolis: Fortress Press, 1991, pp. 337-347.

Pomeroy, Sarah B. *Goddesses, Whores, Wives, and Slaves*. New York: Schocken Books, 1975.

Schulz, Ray R. "A Case for 'President Phoebe' in Romans 16:2." *Lutheran Theological Journal* 24 (1990), pp. 124-127.

Whelan, Caroline F. "*Amica Pauli*: The Role of Phoebe in the Early Church." *Journal for the Study of the New Testament* 49 (1993), pp. 67-85.

Wordelman, Amy L. "Everyday Life: Women in the Period of the New Testament." In *The Women's Bible Commentary, Expanded Edition*. Ed. Carol A. Newsom and Sharon H. Ringe. Louisville: Westminster John Knox Press, 1998, pp. 482-488.

## NOTES

• • • • •

1. Elisabeth Schüssler Fiorenza, *In Memory of Her* (New York: Crossroad, 1985), p. 90; hereafter referred to as *Her*.

2. *Her*, pp. 119 and 121.

3. Elisabeth Schüssler Fiorenza, "Missionaries, Apostles, Coworkers: Romans 16 and the Reconstruction of Women's Early Christian History." *Word and World* 6, #4 (1986): p. 431; hereafter referred to as *Word*.

4. Mary R. Lefkowitz and Maureen B. Fant, *Women's Life in Greece and Rome* (London: Gerald Duckworth and Co., 1982), pp. 141-142.

5. Sarah B. Pomeroy, *Goddesses, Whores, Wives, and Slaves* (New York: Schocken Books, 1975), p. 240.

6. Amy L. Wordelman, "Everyday Life: Women in the Period of the New Testament," in *The Women's Bible Commentary*, ed. Carol A. Newsom and Sharon H. Ringe (London: SPCK and Louisville: Westminster John Knox Press, 1992), p. 395.

7. Caroline F. Whelan, "*Amica Pauli*: The Role of Phoebe in the Early Church," *Journal for the Study of the New Testament* 49 (1993): pp. 73-74.

8. Fiorenza notes that this is most likely, even though it is never explicitly stated.

9. Bernadette J. Brooten, "Women and the Churches in Early Christianity," *Ecumenical Trends* 14 (1985): p. 52; hereafter referred to as *Trends*.

10. Keith A. Gerberding, "Women Who Toil in Ministry, Even As Paul," *Current Trends in Theology and Mission* 18 (1991): p. 189, hereafter referred to as *Toil*; the document referred to is the *Apostolic Constitutions*.

11. *Word*, p. 426.

12. *Toil*, pp. 289-290.

13. *Trends*, p. 52.

14. *Word*, p. 426.

15. Robert Jewett, "Paul, Phoebe, and the Spanish Mission," in *The Social World of Formative Christianity and Judaism: Essays in Tribute to Howard Clark Kee*, eds. Jacob Neusner, Ernest S. Frerich, Peder Borgen, and Richard Horsley (Philadelphia: Fortress Press, 1988).

16. Bernadette Brooten, "Junia . . . Outstanding Among the Apostles (Romans 16:7)," in *Women Priests: A Catholic Commentary on the Vatican Declaration*, eds. Leonard and Arlene Swidler (New York: Paulist Press, 1977), p. 141. She quotes from John Chrysostom (344/54-407) as found in *Epistolan ad Romanos*, Homilia 31, 1 (J.P. Migne, Patrologiae cursus completus series Graeca EPG) 60, 669, f.

𝒯HE SAMARITAN
WOMAN AND US

# We Are Led From the Margin to Mission

*The central focus of the worship environment is water. If there is a large font available, that is best. Otherwise, a large clear bowl of water on a table will be appropriate. A plant could accompany it as a sign of life; or, the bowl could be surrounded by some sand and stones, as a sign of oasis in the parched earth.*

*Ministers:   leader, narrator, Jesus, the Samaritan Woman, some disciples, cantor, and musicians*

*Materials:  large baptismal font or a large table with a bowl of water*

## Introductory Rites

### CALL TO WORSHIP                                      *Please stand*

Leader:     The earth is parched . . . cracked . . . brittle,
            gasping for Living Water.

All:        The parched earth of human hearts that would divide
            Samaritan from Jew, woman from man, black from white,
            that would humiliate a people with a sign at a public
                drinking fountain
            that arrogantly proclaims, "For Whites Only."

Leader:     The parched earth of human eyes,
            shuttered by "this is the way it's always been done,"

distorted by the comfort of privilege,
unable to focus on genuine thirst and hunger.

All:       The parched earth of human mouths,
stuck shut . . . out of fear,
paralyzed by some ancient wound
that still begs for healing.

Leader:    The parched earth of human addictions
that drain and destroy all in their wake,
illusions of answers that never come
at the bottom of an empty glass.

All:       The parched earth of human bodies
wandering the wilderness . . . aimlessly . . . anxiously . . .
in search of a sign . . . some sign, somewhere . . .
any sign of life.

Leader:    Encountered, finally, by the thirst of divine longing
that cannot help but woo just one person
at the well of Living Water

All:       so that an entire people might be set free.

## OPENING HYMN
. . . . . . . . . . . .

"Healing River," text by Fran Minkoff, tune by Fred Hellerman, arr. by Michael Joncas, Appleseed Music, Inc., © 1964.

# Liturgy of the Word
. . . . . . . . . . . . . . . . . . . . . . . . . . . . . . . . . . . . . . . . . . . . . . . . . . . . . .

*Please be seated*

*The Story of the Samaritan Woman, as told by the leader, narrator, Jesus, the Samaritan Woman, and the disciples (see John 4:4-42). The leader, standing off to one side, will offer some brief remarks.*

Leader:    If you were living in the time of Jesus, you would immediately recognize the story of an encounter at a well as a story of betrothal. The servant of Abraham found an appropriate wife for Isaac, son of Abraham and Sarah, at the well of Nahor; her name was Rebekah, and she was "very fair to look upon, a virgin."[1] Jacob, son of Isaac and

Rebekah, met and fell in love with his wife Rachel at the well in Haran.[2] And Moses met his wife Zipporah, the Midianite, at the well in Midian.[3] Remember, too, that Jesus has, by his actions, just declared himself a bridegroom who saved the best wine for last at the wedding feast of Cana.[4] Thus begins our story.

Narrator: Now Jesus had to go through Samaria. So he came to a Samaritan city called Sychar, near the plot of land that Jacob had given to his son Joseph. Jacob's well was there, and Jesus, tired out by his journey, was sitting by the well. It was about noon. A Samaritan woman came to draw water, and Jesus said to her . . .

Jesus: "Give me a drink."

Narrator: (His disciples had gone to the city to buy food.)

Samaritan Woman: "How is it that you, a Jew, ask a drink of me, a woman of Samaria?"

Narrator: (Jews do not share things in common with Samaritans.)

Leader: Indeed, there is intense hatred between Jews and Samaritans. It does not matter that they are family, rooted in Moses and the patriarchs; that may, in fact, make the dispute all the more bitter. To Jews, Samaritans are adulterous people, going after five different gods, from the time that the Assyrians scattered the Samaritans to the four winds. Now this took place over 700 years before the time of Jesus.[5] Four hundred years later the rivalry intensified; the Samaritans built and worshiped at a shrine on Mt. Gerizim, in competition with the Jerusalem Temple. In the late second century before Jesus, this shrine was destroyed by Jewish troops.

Jesus: "If you knew the gift of God, and who it is that is saying to you, 'Give me a drink,' you would have asked him, and he would have given you living water."

Samaritan Woman: "Sir, you have no bucket, and the well is deep. Where do you get that living water? Are you greater than our ancestor Jacob, who gave us the well, and with his sons and his flocks drank from it?"

| | |
|---|---|
| Jesus: | "Everyone who drinks of this water will be thirsty again, but those who drink of the water that I will give them will never be thirsty. The water that I will give will become in them a spring of water gushing up to eternal life." |
| Samaritan Woman: | "Sir, give me this water, so that I may never be thirsty or have to keep coming here to draw water." |
| Jesus: | "Go, call your husband, and come back." |
| Samaritan Woman: | "I have no husband." |
| Jesus: | "You are right in saying, 'I have no husband'; for you have had five husbands, and the one you have now is not your husband. What you have said is true!" |
| Samaritan Woman: | "Sir, I see that you are a prophet. Our ancestors worshiped on this mountain, but you say that the place where people must worship is in Jerusalem." |
| Jesus: | "Woman, believe me, the hour is coming when you will worship the Father neither on this mountain nor in Jerusalem. You worship what you do not know; we worship what we know, for salvation is from the Jews. But the hour is coming, and is now here, where the true worshipers will worship the Father in spirit and truth, for the Father seeks such as these to worship him. God is spirit, and those who worship him must worship in spirit and truth." |
| Samaritan Woman: | "I know that the Messiah is coming," |
| Narrator: | (who is called Christ). |
| Samaritan Woman: | "When he comes, he will proclaim all things to us." |
| Jesus: | "I am he, the one who is speaking to you." |

## MUSICAL RESPONSE

· · · · · · · · · · · · · ·

"Sprinkling Rite" from the "Mass of Creation," refrain and verses 2 and 5, text and tune by Marty Haugen, GIA Publications, Inc., © 1984.

or

"We Shall Draw Water," refrain only, sung twice, text based upon Isaiah 12:3, text and tune by Paul Inwood, published by OCP Publications, © 1986, 1988.

Narrator:    Just then his disciples came. They were astonished that he was speaking with a woman, but no one said, "What do you want?" or, "Why are you speaking with her?"

Leader:    In those days, a rabbi was never allowed to speak with a woman in public, not even his wife.

Narrator:    Then the woman left her water jar and went back to the city. She said to the people,

Samaritan
Woman:    "Come and see a man who told me everything I have ever done! He cannot be the Messiah, can he?"

Narrator:    They left the city and were on their way to him. . . . Meanwhile the disciples were urging him,

Disciples:    "Rabbi, eat something."

Jesus:    "I have food to eat that you do not know about."

Narrator:    So the disciples said to one another,

Disciples:    "Surely no one has brought him something to eat?"

Jesus:    "My food is to do the will of him who sent me and to complete his work. Do you not say, 'Four months more, then comes the harvest'? But I tell you, look around you, and see how the fields are ripe for harvesting. The reaper is already receiving wages and is gathering fruit for eternal life, so that sower and reaper may rejoice together. For here the saying holds true, 'One sows and another reaps.' I sent you to reap that for which you did not labor. Others have labored, and you have entered into their labor."

Narrator:    Many Samaritans from that city believed in him because of the woman's testimony, "He told me everything I have ever done." So when the Samaritans came to him, they asked him to stay with them; and he stayed there two days. And many more believed because of his word. They said to the woman, "It is no longer because of what you said that we believe, for we have heard for ourselves, and we know that this is truly the Savior of the world."

## MUSICAL RESPONSE

. . . . . . . . . . . . . . . .

"Sprinkling Rite" from the "Mass of Creation," refrain and verses 6 and 7.

or

"We Shall Draw Water," refrain only, sung twice.

Narrator:   The Gospel of the Lord.

## BRIEF REFLECTION *(by the Samaritan Woman)*

. . . . . . . . . . . . . . . . . . . . . . . . . . . . . . . . . .

People say I'm tough. And it's true,
my skin is leathered from all those hours
in the searing sun of noonday.
My hide is tough . . . to hide many a wound
from lovers who leave me . . .
and neighbors who shun me.
They've conveniently forgotten how many times
their ancestors—and mine—prowled after false gods themselves . . .
though I couldn't have told you that 'til now.

Oh, I knew I was on the prowl for love.
But . . . I had no idea how thirsty I really was
for a look of delight, a touch of respect, a love that would last.
But that day at the well . . . with Jesus . . . changed everything.
I was an open book to him,
and he laughed with delight at my assertiveness.
Yes, he told me so. He told me everything, in fact.
At this place of Living Water he wooed and won me . . .
and betrothed me to his God.

Imagine! Me, a Samaritan and a woman!
I had no need of my water jug any longer,
for now I, myself, became a vessel of Living Water,
a conduit of the good news to my people with the pointed fingers.
"Come and see!" My voice brimmed with Living Water
and could not be contained.
Yes, it splashed all over the people who had rejected me,
quenching our thirst and setting us free.

*Silence*

Leader: Each of us is the Samaritan Woman. She is the one who spent most of her adult life in and out of prison. Addicted and HIV positive. Until she met someone who brought her Living Water, who cared about her . . . unconditionally. Now she is in recovery, working with women in prison, that they might know they are worth something.

Or, she is a woman in the Roman Catholic church, called by God to be a priest. And she thirsts to proclaim the Good News in a church that solemnly declares it has no authority to ordain a woman.

Or, she is a woman who happens to be homosexual. She has borne the heat of the day with questions like, "What would my family say? Will my friends still love me? And, what do I make of my church, who says I'm 'disordered'?" But she is coming to some peace, having found God, like a spring in the wilderness; she knows that God is so much bigger than most of us can possibly imagine.

Take a few moments of quiet, now, and listen to the voice of the Samaritan Woman in the depths of your very being. Where are you thirsty? And, where have you found a thirsty God seeking you out?

*During these few moments, instrumental music is played. It might be "Song Over the Waters," which is named below during the ritual, or some other appropriate music.*

## Ritual of Coming to the Water

### INVITATION TO COME TO THE LIVING WATER

Leader: Water has power. Consider this story.[6] A man had a cellar that would fill with water every now and again, and nothing he tried could keep it out. So, he finally brought in an engineer, who told him that there was an underground stream that flowed directly under the house's foundation. The only solution was to open the cellar and dig a trench in the floor that would allow the water to flow, unhindered. When he did that, the water would sing—as only the gentle sound of living water can do—filling the entire house with music.

God is like that. God is an irrepressible, powerful force, just waiting to bubble up in joyful song at the foundation of our lives. If only we don't stop the flow. Or, try to deny the "problem." Or, try to force God into a tiny trickle instead of a life-giving stream. In a moment, we will be invited to this Living Water, which we will now bless together.

## BLESSING OF THE WATER

All:    Sung refrain of "Song Over the Waters," text and tune by Marty Haugen, GIA Publications, Inc., © 1987.

*Instrumental music begins, with the Woman inviting people to extend an arm in blessing:*

Samaritan
Woman:    O God of irrepressible life, bless this water, we pray, that it might be filled with the power that you alone have, to open up a future for us now, a pathway beyond the limits of human imagination.

All:    *Sing refrain.*

## COMING TO THE WATER

Leader:    As you wish, you may come forward now and reverence or touch the water in whatever way is appropriate for you. Then you may either go to the Samaritan Woman, or myself, and say something like, "I am in need of Living Water." You will then hear words of blessing, "(*Name*), be filled with the power of the Living Water, the power of your baptism."

*Musicians continue to sing the entire hymn, "Song Over the Waters."*

# Closing Rites

## BLESSING / SENDING FORTH

*Please stand*

*Each "half" of the assembly faces the other, offering an arm in blessing with these words:*

Left:      The power of Christ is irrepressible.

Right:     The power of the Living Water will quench all thirst.

Left:      The power of our baptism can become a river of life,

Right:     connecting, transforming, enlivening,
           refreshing, reconciling all in its wake.

Left:      Go forth, in the power of the Living Water

Right:     Go forth, in the power of the Living Water

Left:      to heal and transform, comfort and challenge,

Right:     to heal and transform, comfort and challenge.

All:       Amen! Yes, let it be! Amen!

## CLOSING HYMN

*Please stand*

"Sing a New Church," text by Delores Dufner, O.S.B., Sisters of St. Benedict, published by OCP Publications. Music from J. Wyeth's *Repository of Sacred Music*, Pt. II, 1813.

## NOTES

1.   See Genesis 24:16.

2.   See Genesis 29:1-20.

3.   See Exodus 2:16-22.

4.   See John 2:1-12.

5.   See 2 Kings 17:13-34.

6.   This story, written by Thomas Troeger, appeared in the April 2001 issue of *Lectionary Homiletics*, "Themes for the Season: Futile Strategies for Resisting God" (Midlothian, VA: Lectionary Homiletics, Inc., 2001).

# The Samaritan Woman
## Encounters Living Water

The sun was beating down mercilessly, parching the earth, blinding the eye. A woman bore the brunt of the heat of that day, with the aid of a walking stick. But she walked, sure-footed and courageous, head held high for the dignity of her people, her eyes fixed on the living water. She walked, slowly but surely, past a row of state troopers, all white, all carrying guns, cocked and ready to shoot. She walked, slowly but surely, a black woman, now one hundred years of age, who had suffered one too many indignities, who had been born a slave but who would no longer be kept from an all-white drinking fountain. She walked to that fountain . . . bent down . . . and drank deeply of that cool, refreshing water that leaped up within her like a fountain of everlasting life. Then she turned, a woman now straight and tall; she faced those state troopers with a look of the deepest satisfaction, and headed back to her people.

That scene provides the ending of the movie *The Autobiography of Miss Jane Pittman*, based upon the 1971 book of the same name, by Ernest J. Gaines. It is the story of rural life in Louisiana at the dawn of the civil rights movement. It is a story with many of the same themes—in our day and age—as the powerful story of the Samaritan Woman for every age. It is a story of boundary breaking, of destroying the walls of imagined difference. It is a story of empowerment and mission. It is a story of inclusive discipleship, of the least likely serving as the vessel of mission. It is a story of God wooing the beloved, for the sake of winning over an entire nation. It is, for Christians, the story of what it means to be baptized, to be filled with the power of Living Water for the sake of God's vision in our world. A brief look at each of these themes will reveal some of the depth and power of this story.

## BOUNDARY BREAKING

Jews (the people native to Judah, in the south) and Samaritans (the people who claimed the land in between Judah and Galilee to the north, who had been part of the Northern Kingdom) hated each other. They were family, descendants of Moses and the patriarchs, but the Samaritans believed only in the Torah. Furthermore, the Samaritans were among the people defeated and scattered into exile in 722 B.C.E. by the Assyrians. The Jews in the south, who held on to their king and kingdom until 587 B.C.E., viewed the resulting Samaritan intermarriage and idolatry with particular disdain. In their view, the Samaritans had gone chasing after five different gods, or *ba'als*, destroying their covenant relationship with Yahweh.[1] By the fourth century B.C.E., competition intensified over the "right" place to worship God: the rebuilt Temple of Jerusalem on Mt. Zion or the Samaritan temple on Mt. Gerizim, near this very well. Finally, in the second century before Jesus, hatred erupted, as first Samaritans supported Syrian rulers against the Jews, and then the Jewish high priest destroyed the Samaritan temple at Mt. Gerizim in 128 B.C.E. Jesus shatters this enmity, this presumed difference worthy of hatred, in stretching his arm across the Jew-Samaritan divide.[2]

But, this is not the only boundary he destroys. When the disciples return from their shopping trip for food, they are "astonished that he was speaking with a *woman*," though they do not voice their questions. After all, the rabbinic teaching is clear, "The wise men say: 'Who speaks much with a woman draws down misfortune on himself, neglects the words of the law, and finally earns hell'!"[3] It can only be noted that religious traditions today—some more than others—continue to struggle with this male-female divide. Indeed, some scripture scholarship is still infected with put-downs of this woman, in some cases refusing to see the depth of theological discussion she enters into with Jesus. She wants to know, is he greater than Jacob? Could he be, perhaps, the prophet like Moses, only greater than Moses, the one they have all been waiting for?[4] By revealing everything in her past, Jesus hits his mark with her. She does not disappoint, but comes right to the theological point. Where is God to be worshiped? Yes, Jesus is right; she is exactly the one capable of hearing and bearing his Good News, the revelation that he is the ancient "I am," the messiah that alone can satisfy the thirst of people for life and meaning.

## EMPOWERMENT AND MISSION

This is a story of transformation and mission. It is the story of a woman coming to belief, leaving her former life (the water jar) behind, venturing forth to people who have probably shunned her (she customarily drew water in the heat of the day, when nobody else was around), and extending to them the classic call to discipleship, "Come and see." She is already an answer to the prayer that Jesus will pray to God at the Last Supper, a prayer for all those "who will believe in me through their word."[5] And she completes her mission by connecting

Jesus with the Samaritan people, who ask him to "remain" (abide, in Johannine terminology) with them, and who come to a deeper level of faith because of direct contact with Jesus. In his conversation with the disciples, Jesus hungers for just such a mission. He can almost taste the harvest, ripe and ready for picking, but the disciples have no idea what he is talking about.

## INCLUSIVE DISCIPLESHIP—THE LEAST LIKELY AS A VESSEL OF LIVING WATER

Who would ever have chosen a Samaritan and a woman—with a questionable background—as a model of discipleship? The scripture scholar Pheme Perkins notes that there is no satisfactory explanation of the five husbands.[6] And yet, Sandra Schneiders makes a strong case that these "husbands," "*ba'als*" in Hebrew, represent the false gods of the Samaritan people.[7] She notes that the exchange regarding her "husbands" takes place in the midst of a theological discussion on proper worship. Furthermore, Jesus' pronouncement that she "has no husband" is a classic prophetic denunciation of false worship; Jesus simply states the fact, and the woman recognizes its truth.

In John's Gospel, Jesus is very comfortable calling this woman to discipleship. Indeed, she is like the disciples called in the synoptic gospels, who leave net and fishing boat behind to follow Jesus. She is the only person in the gospels to bring a whole people to him. And, she is also the subject of some tension in this regard, as is evident in the reaction of the disciples to Jesus' conversation with her. The ease with which Jesus called this woman has yet to be duplicated among a number of his followers.

## A BETROTHAL STORY, GOD WOOING THE BELOVED

The people hearing this story for the first time would recognize the signs of betrothal. There is an encounter at a well. The servant of Abraham found an appropriate wife for Isaac, son of Abraham and Sarah, at the well of Nahor. She became the matriarch Rebekah. Jacob, son of Isaac and Rebekah, met and immediately fell in love with his wife Rachel at the well in Haran. And Moses met his wife Zipporah at the well in Midian. Jesus had just recently declared his intentions as bridegroom at the wedding feast of Cana, by saving the best wine for last. And now he woos the Samaritan Woman, symbolic of her entire people, into covenant fidelity with the God of Spirit and Truth. Immediately after this encounter with the Samaritans, Jesus will return to Cana to bring to belief someone altogether outside the people of Israel, the pagan royal official, whose son he heals.[8] In this "Cana to Cana" section, Jesus has wooed the beloved, and they have responded.

## A STORY OF THE MEANING OF BAPTISM

The Samaritan Woman, like all humanity, is thirsty for life, belonging, and meaning. She is plunged into the One who thirsts for us—Living Water—and is transformed, capable now of bringing an entire nation to the Water she has discovered. She is seeker, disciple, missionary, reconciler, vessel of Living Water to all who thirst, beloved daughter, person of dignity and responsibility. She is all that a baptized person is intended to become. As Paul proclaimed regarding baptism, "There is no longer Jew or Greek, there is no longer slave or free, there is no longer male and female; for all of you are one in Christ Jesus."[9] The story of the Samaritan Woman is a promise that the church has yet to keep.

## SOME RESOURCES

Brown, Raymond E., S.S. *The Gospel According to John*. Garden City, NY: Doubleday & Company, Inc., 1966.

Brown, Raymond E., S.S., Joseph A. Fitzmyer, S.J., and Roland E. Murphy, O. Carm., Editors. *The New Jerome Biblical Commentary*. Englewood Cliffs, NJ: Prentice Hall, 1990.

Meehan, Bridget Mary. *Praying With Women of the Bible*. Liguori, MO: Liguori/ Triumph, 1998.

O'Day, Gail R. "John" in *Women's Bible Commentary, Expanded Edition with Apocrypha*, Editors Carol A. Newsom and Sharon H. Ringe. Louisville, KY: Westminster John Knox Press, 1998, pp. 381-393.

Pearson, Helen Bruch. *Do What You Have the Power to Do: Studies of Six New Testament Women*. Nashville: Upper Room Books, 1992.

Schneiders, Sandra M. *Written That You May Believe: Encountering Jesus in the Fourth Gospel*. New York: The Crossroad Publishing Company, 1999.

## NOTES

1.  See the scriptural account of this idolatry in 2 Kings 17:13-34.

2.  Several scholars today, including Sandra Schneiders, in her *Written That You May Believe* (New York: Crossroad Publishing Co., 1999), believe that this story was probably not part of the life of the historical Jesus. Rather, it came out of reflection by the Johannine community, and its purpose was to legitimize the evangelization of Samaria for Christ.

3.  Helen Bruch Pearson quotes from the *Mishnah Aboth* 1, 5 in her *Do What You Have the Power to Do* (Nashville: Upper Room Books, 1992), p. 144.

4.  This prophet like Moses had been promised in Deuteronomy 18:18-19.

5.  See John 17:20.

6.  See "The Gospel According to John" in *The New Jerome Biblical Commentary*, Ed. Raymond E. Brown, S.S., Joseph A. Fitzmyer, S.J., and Roland E. Murphy, O. Carm. (Englewood Cliffs, NJ: Prentice Hall, 1990), p. 957.

7.  See Sandra Schneiders, *Written That You May Believe* (New York: Crossroad Publishing Co., 1999), pp. 137-148.

8.  Sandra Schneiders offers a caution here in her book *Written That You May Believe*, p. 147. If the image of the bridegroom God is taken literally, it can fall into the trap of the male God and the female believer, cementing gender inequality.

9.  See Galatians 3:28.

# three

# SARAH AND HAGAR

## We Struggle for Vision Amid Systems That Divide

·····································································

*Everyone will receive a stone on the way in. Central to the worship space is a table with an elevated unrolled scroll on which is written, "Thus says God, 'I am with you; I am for you.'" On one side of the scroll is a basket with paper hearts (clean hearts), on the other, an empty basket (for the stones during the ritual). Next to this basket is a large candle.*

*The "feel" of this liturgy is one of lament, of questioning, and of providing a space for reflection and challenge. It is a call for us, who are heirs of Abraham and Sarah, to "see." It is a call to a change of heart from any hardness of heart to a "clean heart." The story, as told by Sarah, Hagar, and the narrator, is meant to incorporate both scripture and homily. It will draw from Genesis and offer a reflection on the biblical text. As the story begins, Sarah and Hagar are far apart physically. At a certain point, when the narrator "drops out," they come face to face. This liturgy may be celebrated at any time but is very appropriately celebrated during Lent.*

*Ministers:   leader, narrator, Sarah, Hagar, cantor, and musicians*

*Materials:   table, two baskets, scroll, stones, paper hearts*

# Introductory Rites

## WELCOME *(Leader)*

Welcome, everyone. Tonight we are invited to "see," to lament, to question, and to be challenged to a change of heart. For tonight we are immersed into God's covenant with us. And we must begin by traveling to distant shores: to a time nearly 4000 years ago, and to the culture of the ancient Near East. It was a culture where men could have more than one wife, where men alone carried the sign of God's covenant, circumcision. Women were regarded as objects . . . objects of affection, and as property . . . something to be had. It was a culture where women were meant to serve men by having boys who would become men, a sign of God's everlasting favor. Slavery was a given and oppression was layered, especially if the slave was a woman with dark skin, who came from outside the ranks of the chosen people.

As we listen to Sarah and Hagar, two of our earliest ancestors in faith, we are invited to leave the familiar behind, to see from other points of view, and to ask ourselves, "What does God's covenant mean for us today?" But first, we begin by preparing our hearts to become fertile ground for God's faithful love.

## OPENING HYMN                                       *Please stand*

"Kyrie" from the *Mass of Remembrance*, tune by Marty Haugen, GIA Publications, Inc., © 1987.

## OPENING PRAYER *(All)*

O God of every age, eternal with us and for us,
you alone can eliminate the distance
of time and space, conflict and culture,
so that we may gather as family with Sarah and Hagar.
Create in us a sacred space,
a place of reverence for Sarah and Hagar,
for ourselves, and all our sisters and brothers.
Hollow out in us
a womb to birth Wisdom and Understanding,
so that the land we inherit becomes holy ground.
In your holy name, we pray. Amen.

# Liturgy of the Word

. . . . . . . . . . . . . . . . . . . . . . . . . . . . . . . . . . . . . . . . . . . . . . . . .

JEREMIAH 34:31-34 *(Narrator)*                    *Please be seated*

. . . . . . . . . . . . . . . . . . . . . . .

PSALM 51

. . . . . . . .

"Create in Me," text by David Haas (based on Psalm 51), tune by David Haas, GIA Publications, Inc., © 1987.

STORIES OF THE COVENANT
*(told by Sarah and Hagar, based on Genesis 12-23)*

. . . . . . . . . . . . . . . . . . . . . . . . . . . . . . . . . . . . . . . . . . .

Narrator:  Let's be clear. From the point of view of the writer, this story is about Abraham. It's about the ancestry of the Hebrew nation and how God called Abram, "exalted one," to become Abraham, "father of a multitude of nations." But there's more to the story than this. For Sarah, it's a story of a cherished promise . . . new life in an impossible situation, at an impossible age. But the wilderness intrudes, for God's promise is spoken, not to her, but to her husband. For Hagar, it's a direct promise of God, "I will so greatly multiply your offspring that they cannot be counted for multitude."[1] But the wilderness literally haunts Hagar . . . with servitude . . . a disturbing promise of ongoing enmity . . . and even a shift in the promise from Hagar to Ishmael, son of Abraham. But, there's more to the story than this. For God's word is alive. Piercing. Penetrating. Probing. Promising. Enduring. Summoning us all, as descendants of Abraham, Sarah, and Hagar, from unresolved tension and terror to profound sisterhood and brotherhood. It is for us, as it was for our ancestors in faith, a story of beginning again. Listen, then, as our story begins with Sarah and Hagar.

Sarah:  I was considered very beautiful, even at sixty-five years of age.[2] For that was when our story began, mine and Abraham's, you might say. I remember that day like it was yesterday *(with a nostalgic air)*. Abram came running to me like a youngster, "Sarai! Sarai! You'll never guess what happened! God spoke to me! To *me*! And God promised me blessings . . . that I would be 'a great nation,' that my name would be great, that in me 'all the families of the earth shall be blessed.'[3] All we have to do is pull up our tent stakes and go . . . to a land that God will show us."

It was exciting, then. An adventure. It never occurred to me, then, to question why God didn't speak to me as well. It all seemed simple enough. So, off we went, with Lot, Abram's nephew, and all the people attached to us, the people who looked up to us.

Trust in God came easy then. But life would not be so simple. Oh, we made it to Canaan, all right, but Abram is not one to settle down. So on we went . . . to the desert, the Negeb . . . and to famine. That's when our first real test came, for we ended up in Egypt. Abram insisted that I was so beautiful that the Pharaoh would want me, and Abram's life would be in danger. Wouldn't I just say I was his sister? And agree to be the Pharaoh's wife?

For the very first time, I felt used! By my very own husband! And the hurt went very deep, because Abram had always been so good to me. Always setting up my tent first, whenever we came to a new place.[4] Treating me like a princess, for that is what my name means. But I kept silent, that time. After all, what was I to do? It was how things were, but something felt very wrong.

Cantor: *Refrain, sung twice, led by the cantor: "In My Day of Fear," tune "Distant Oaks," words based on psalm 56 and music, The Iona Community, GIA Publications, Inc., © 1993.*

Narrator: I am told that people who are very beautiful in scripture are also considered holy.[5] Is that how you see yourself? And, did God hear your cry?

Sarah: Well, there was a time when I had felt close to God, certainly when we started out. But, at that moment, I was just feeling like a pawn . . . in the hands of Abram *and* of God. And yet, I suppose you *could* say that God heard me. After all, the next thing we knew, the Pharaoh was being inflicted with plagues because of Abram's scheme. And, the

Pharaoh was so impressed by this that he let us go, with more possessions than ever! We had so much, in fact, that we had to separate from Lot, so there would be enough land for us all. But, I was starting to feel very left out.

Oh, the promises of God continued. But they were always for Abram, spoken only to Abram. Land, as far as the eye could see.[6] Land "from the river of Egypt to the great river, the river Euphrates."[7] Offspring as numerous as "the dust of the earth."[8] Or, as many as the stars, on a starlit night.[9] Where was *I* in all this? Empty. Barren of a son who would honor me in my old age, and give glee to Abram, who had been so sure of God's promises. Were these promises empty . . . barren? It had been ten long years since we had first pulled up stakes. Where *was* God, anyway?

It was time for me to take matters into my own hands! I saw my slave-girl Hagar and said to Abram, "Go in to my slave-girl; maybe I will finally have a child by her."[10] At that point, I was thinking more about my enduring shame of being barren than about fulfilling the promises of God, I will tell you.

Hagar:    Yes, this is where I come in. And I had nothing to say about what happened next, absolutely nothing. Did it matter that I was young, feisty, and eager for life? And that Abraham was eighty-five years old and withered by then? No. It was how things were in our day. It was perfectly all right, for the ones making the laws, at least, that a servant girl could become another wife and a surrogate mother. My child would belong to Sarai; that's how it worked.[11] And, indeed, I became pregnant, but that's not the end of the story. It is only the beginning. For I saw something Sarai had not anticipated. Sarai, my "mistress," was *beneath* me; she could not do this very thing that was happening inside me. I knew it, and she knew it. She saw the change in me and began to afflict me and oppress me harshly.[12] So, I ran away. Where was I going? Away from her. That's all I knew. And I ended up in the wilderness, on the way to Shur.

Cantor:    *Refrain, sung twice: "In My Day of Fear."*

Narrator: What happened, Hagar? Did God hear your cry?

Hagar: It's not so clear; it's not a simple "Yes" or "No." Yes, God found me by a spring of water in the wilderness. Yes, God saw me and called me by name, which Sarai and Abram had never bothered to do. *And*, God made *me* a promise, not unlike the one I had heard Abram speak of so often, "I will so greatly multiply your offspring that they cannot be counted for multitude."[13] Not only that, but God spoke of the son I was carrying, "you shall call him Ishmael, for the Lord has given heed to your affliction."[14]

I was so grateful that *I* named *God*. "You are El-roi," the God who sees.[15] But, God also described my son's life in terms of my own, at odds with everyone, even with his kin. And, worst of all, God sent me back, "to submit to my mistress Sarai"! Was it because I had no idea who I was or where I was going? Was it because God's promise was too good for me to hear? Did I even imagine that I deserved to be sent back? Had I "bought into" the male system of my time, somehow craving security more than freedom? Did I believe that Ishmael would be safe back there? Was it because God knew I could become a strong survivor, that God would always make a way for me where there was no way?

I don't know. I can only say this. I went back, feeling much older, but somehow stronger. Able to endure whatever came along over the next thirteen years—until everything would change again.

Sarah: Yes, my time finally came! Or, should I say, *God's* time for me finally came? Anyway, I knew something was up on the day that Abram came running to me again, like that day twenty-four years earlier, just before we first set out. "Sarah! Sarah! (He was saying my name differently now.) It's time! God just spoke to me again, and it's the same promise, but now everything is different! God will do the impossible for us—I'm sure of it—for this is what God said: 'No longer shall your name be Abram, but your name shall be Abraham. . . . As for Sarai your wife, you shall not call her Sarai, but Sarah shall be her name. I will bless her, and moreover I will give you a son by her. I will bless her, and she shall give rise to nations; kings of people shall come from her.'"[16]

Impossible, I thought! Just another promise, I thought! Until the day came—not long after, actually—when three travelers showed up at our tent. Would you believe they were messengers from God? The promise was true! I was eavesdropping from my tent when God announced to Abraham that we would have a son in due season. I laughed, right out loud! To enjoy the pleasure of sex, at my age?! But my laughter was real, a *huge* belly laugh, for Isaac was born right on schedule.[17] And I was thrilled.

Except. . . . If laughter can be healing, it was not so for me. Maybe the wait had been too long and the hurt too deep. I don't know. But on the day when Isaac was weaned, something snapped inside me. I felt threatened, angry, hurt, jealous. There was Isaac, playing with Ishmael. After all, Ishmael *was* Abraham's first-born son. Would he take my son's place? Would he become the son of promise, after all? That could not happen! I would not let it happen! So I *commanded* Abraham to send him and Hagar away, where they would never be seen or heard from again. He didn't say much . . . he wasn't happy about it—he was agitated, in fact—but he did as I said. He sent them off early one morning with only a skin of water and some bread. . . . (*At this point, the Narrator moves away and Hagar comes up into the Narrator's place, so that the women are face to face.*)

Hagar:     As for me, there's not much more to be said. Except this. Sarah, do you have any idea what it felt like out there, wandering aimlessly in the wilderness? With death hovering like a menacing bird? Nearly abandoning my very own son because I couldn't bear to watch him die? Nearly despairing of God's goodness, even feeling that God had all but abandoned me? Or, at the very least, believing that God had come to prefer my son to me. For this is what I heard, "What troubles you, Hagar? Do not be afraid; for God has heard the voice of the boy where he is. Come, lift up the boy and hold him fast with your hand, for I will make a great nation of him."[18]

But, something in me would not give up. For I had learned this much, that things are not always as they appear. And I had enough stamina and belief in my God to keep on going. To find an Egyptian wife for Ishmael and make sure that Egyptian blood would flow through my descendants' veins. To see God's promise through. And, in the end, to believe that I really did matter to God.

Sarah: (*After a great pause*) At the time, you know, I did what I felt I had to do. After all, the important thing in my time was for the male line to continue. The important thing was for the rightful heir to inherit the land. That was a sign of God's favor; that's all we knew. And yet, Hagar, now I can begin to see . . . to see more. For I felt abandoned, too, by my very own husband. When I found out, after the fact, that Abraham had taken my only son, my child of laughter, up the mountain to kill him, thinking he was doing the will of *God*, of all things, I was heartbroken. After all these years, what kind of a God did he think he was following? Did he really believe that *God* wanted to him to do that? I hadn't been privy to all those conversations between God and Abraham, but I knew better than that!

In the end, of course, God intervened. But, I died soon afterward, for my heart was never the same. Is that the kind of pain you suffered after I banished you? Is there something else I might have done? (*Pause*) What would have happened if I could have seen you as a sister . . . instead of a rival?

Hagar: And yet, God was with me, more than I knew, more than I could see.

Sarah: And yet, God was with me, more than I knew, more than I could see.

Hagar: God surprised me, beyond my wildest imagination, with a son of my own, the father of a nation.

Sarah: God surprised me, beyond my wildest imagination, with a son of my own, the father of a nation.

Hagar: Freedom was within my reach, but beyond my grasp.[19]

| | |
|---|---|
| Sarah: | Freedom was within my reach, but beyond my grasp. |
| Hagar: | For I could not see beyond the limits of my day . . . that the male line, through the preferred son, is what matters most. |
| Sarah: | For I could not see beyond the limits of my day . . . that the male line, through the preferred son, is what matters most. |
| Hagar: | And yet, this I know: I mattered to God. O Eternal One, O God of every nation, give wholeness and strength to my descendants, as numerous as the stars. |
| Sarah: | And yet, this I know: I mattered to God. O Eternal One, O God of every generation, give healing and strength to my descendants, as numerous as the stars. |

Refrain, sung once, with Hagar: "In My Day of Fear."

Refrain, sung once, with Sarah: "In My Day of Fear."

*Silence*

## Ritual of Seeing

• • • • • • • • • • • • • • • • • • • • • • • • • • • • • • • • • • • • • • • • • • • • •

PREPARATION (*Leader*)

• • • • • • • • • • • • • • • • • •

Our covenant God is with us and for us, continually calling us to see beyond the limits that our culture and/or church may impose. Some questions come to mind. With whom do I most identify in the story just told? Where am I most challenged . . . and what does that ask of me? It is in looking back and taking stock that we begin to see where our vision has been clouded by the systems of which we are a part. Where have I bumped up against the limits of my tradition . . . or where have I limited others? And what does that ask of me? How can I become part of healing the wounds of division? Please take a few moments to name your vision of God's covenant today . . . and any nudge you experience toward a change of heart.

## MUSIC DURING THE RITUAL

Psalm 51: "Create in Me," text by David Haas (based on Psalm 51), tune by David Haas, GIA Publications, Inc., © 1987.

## INVITATION *(Leader)*

As you are ready, come forward with your stone and pick up a heart from the basket. You will be leaving behind anything that stands in the way of God's vision for us. This heart represents God's vision in you and will be a reminder of your ability to see ever more of what God has in mind for us. Then, in whatever way is comfortable, reverence the Covenant scroll and pick up your "clean heart."

## MUSIC DURING THE RITUAL

"Deep Within," text and tune by David Haas, GIA Publications, Inc., © 1987.

or

"Healer of Our Every Ill," text and tune by Marty Haugen, GIA Publications, Inc., © 1987.

# Closing Rites

## INVITATION TO COVENANT LIFE *(Leader)*          *Please stand*

Renewed in God's heart, we prepare now to go forth with God's blessing to seek out and serve our sisters and our brothers. As we do so, please extend an arm in blessing on all here gathered, believing that these arms are supported by the outstretched arm of our eagle-winged God, who has brought us to the divine within us all.

## BLESSING *(All)*

O God of Sarah and Hagar,
O God of every race, creed, color, gender, and hue,
enduring God who is with us and for us,
summon us forth,
from comfort to conversion,

from passivity to passion,
from fondness for others into the furnace of your love.
Forge us into a sign of your covenant,
that we might become a blessing to all.
This we ask in your holy name,
O God, Beyond All Names. Amen.

## CLOSING HYMN                                   *Please stand*
• • • • • • • • • • • • • • •

"God, Beyond All Names," Bernadette Farrell, published by OCP Publications, © 1990.

## NOTES
• • • • •

1.  See Genesis 16:10.

2.  See Genesis 12:4, 14; we learn elsewhere (Gn 17:17) that Sarah is ten years younger than Abraham.

3.  See Genesis 12:2-3.

4.  Irene Nowell, O.S.B., points this out in her book, *Women in the Old Testament* (Collegeville, MN: The Liturgical Press, 1997), p. 4; hereafter referred to as Nowell. According to her, this is part of rabbinic tradition.

5.  Nowell, p. 5. Note, for example, Joseph (Gn 39:6), David (1 Sm 16:12), Tamar (2 Sm 13:1), Abishag (1 Kgs 1:3-4).

6.  See Genesis 13:14-15.

7.  See Genesis 15:18.

8.  See Genesis 13:16.

9.  See Genesis 15:5-6.

10. See Genesis 16:2.

11. Nowell, p. 7. It was a Mesopotamian custom (i.e., the law codes from Nuzi) for the child to be considered the child of the wife; but, in this case, Sarai never really claimed him. When Sarai handed Hagar over to Abram, she gave Hagar as a wife (the Hebrew is *ishshah*), not a concubine, to Abram.

12. It is the Exodus in reverse. Sarai, the Hebrew, afflicted Hagar, the Egyptian.

13. See Genesis 16:10. Hagar is the only woman in scripture to receive the same promise as a man.

14. See Genesis 16:11. This is part of the very first birth announcement in scripture; the name Ishmael means "God heeds."

15.  See Genesis 16:13. Hagar is the only person in scripture to give a name to God.

16.  See Genesis 17:5a, 15-16. The sign of this covenant was to be circumcision for all males; newborn males were to be circumcised when they were eight days old.

17.  The name Isaac means "he laughs."

18.  See Genesis 21:17b-18.

19.  I owe this idea to Renita Weems, from the chapter on Sarah and Hagar ("A Mistress, A Maid, and No Mercy") in her book, *Just a Sister Away* (San Diego, CA: LuraMedia, 1988), p. 13. She refers here to Hagar.

# The Covenant, As Told in Genesis 12–25 and Experienced by Sarah and Hagar

In the beginning, God created the heavens and the earth out of darkness and chaos. And God proclaimed that it was good. Finally, when God created humans, male and female, in the divine image, God sighed in delight, "Ahhh, very good!" But, many long generations later, chaos and confusion reigned once again. For the people had sinned. They had even tried to "make a name" for themselves by building "a tower with its top in the heavens."[1] So, God confused their language and "scattered them abroad from there over the face of all the earth," and the tower became known as the Tower of Babel.[2] But, God had made an everlasting promise, a covenant with one righteous man, Noah, and with his descendants and with every creature on the earth. Whenever a rainbow appeared in the sky, it would be a reminder to God that "never again shall there be a flood to destroy the earth," as there was in the time of Noah.[3]

God made good on the promise, for God began again with one of Noah's descendants. Abram, "Exalted One," was in the line of Shem, one of the sons of Noah. One day, God called Abram out of his native land, Ur (in Mesopotamia) of the Chaldeans, "to the land that I will show you."[4] Thus begins the saga of Abraham and his descendants, the people of Israel, the story of God beginning again. This story is told in Genesis 11:10–25:34. In its present form, it is the story of God's everlasting covenant with Abram, and how he became Abraham, "Father of a multitude of nations." But scripture has a surplus of meaning, and it is the purpose of these brief comments to begin to explore some of that surplus, especially for women, through the eyes of Sarah and Hagar.

But first, the outline of the story is this. God summons Abram with a multitude of promises besides the land: "I will make of you a great nation, and I will bless you, and make your name great, so that you will be a blessing. I will bless those who bless you, and the one who curses you I will curse; and in you all the families of the earth shall be blessed."[5] Abram leaves with his wife, Sarai, his nephew, Lot, and all the people attached to them. But, suspense is in the air, for Abram is already seventy-five years old and Sarai is sixty-five and barren.[6] And yet, God's promises to Abram multiply: 1) the land of Canaan to Abram and his offspring forever, with offspring as numerous as "the dust of the earth,"[7] 2) descendants as numerous as the stars, from his "very own issue,"[8] 3) land "from the river of Egypt to the great river, the river Euphrates," as sworn by God through an ancient ceremony,[9] and 4) an everlasting covenant "to be God to you and to your offspring after you."[10]

At the time of this last promise, Abram is ninety-nine years old; and God commands Abram to keep this covenant by circumcising every male among him, including those of future generations when they are eight days old. Only this time, it is clear that something is about to happen, for God changes Abram's name to Abraham and Sarai's name to Sarah. And *she* figures prominently in the promises for the first time. "I will bless her, and moreover I will give you a son by her. I will bless her, and she shall give rise to nations; kings of people shall come from her."[11] Impossible as it seems, and after both Abraham and Sarah have had a good laugh over this, God makes good on this promise. "Sarah conceived and bore Abraham a son in his old age. . . . Abraham gave the name Isaac to his son whom Sarah bore him. And Abraham circumcised his son Isaac when he was eight days old, as God had commanded him. Abraham was a hundred years old when his son Isaac was born to him."[12]

The name Isaac means laughter. But, all is not laughter for Abraham, Sarah, and Sarah's "slave-girl," Hagar, the Egyptian. The trouble had started fifteen years earlier. Not only had Sarai been unable to conceive, she could not conceive a way in which God's promises would ever be fulfilled. So, taking matters into her own hands, she decided to "obtain children" through Hagar, an acceptable custom of her day.[13] She hands over Hagar to Abram as another wife; and Hagar immediately becomes pregnant with a child that Sarai can claim as her own. This is a recipe for trouble, and trouble there is. Hagar sees that Sarai is "slight" in her eyes; in return, Sarai afflicts Hagar, and Hagar runs away.[14] Alone, out in the wilderness, Hagar is the recipient of the Bible's first birth announcement. God proclaims to Hagar that she is to bear a son and name him Ishmael. This son will continue to live out her story, at odds with his kin; but he will also be the beginning of a great multitude of offspring for her.[15] In response to a promise not unlike one given to Abram, Hagar names God, "El-roi," meaning "God who sees." Obviously a special person, she is the only one in scripture who dares to name God.

But the story does not end there. Indeed, it is only the beginning of more trouble. For God immediately sends her back, to "submit" to Sarai. And, the conflict between the two women only intensifies, even after the birth of Isaac. In fact, on the very day of Isaac's weaning, Sarah erupts in a jealous rage. Will Ishmael inherit with Isaac? She orders Abraham to banish "this slave woman with her son"; and Abraham—distressed at this turn of events—reluctantly agrees.[16] But God consoles Abraham that "it is through Isaac that offspring shall be named for you. As for the son of the slave woman, I will make a nation of him also, because he is your offspring."[17]

What follows is the troubling trauma of Hagar wandering the wilderness.[18] *This* time though, God hears and responds to her second near-death experience. The divine concern and covenant are now for Ishmael. But trauma leaves its mark on Sarah, as well, in the so-called "testing" of Abraham.[19] How could she ever comprehend that her lifetime companion could sacrifice Isaac, the child of laughter? In the end, God intervenes to save this beloved son; but the next we hear of Sarah, she dies at age 127. In the end, the divine promises to Abraham are kept; the multitude of descendants has begun. For Isaac marries Rebekah, from among Abraham's kin, not from among the Canaanites. And their younger son, Jacob, the son of favor, steals the birthright from the older, Esau.

That is the story as told in scripture, mainly from Abraham's point of view. But we have questions about the trouble, some of it seemingly at the hand of God.[20] Feminist scholars put the bottom-line question this way: If God is a God of liberation, setting the people free to serve God and God's people, why do some stories seem to reflect a God of oppression, or even abuse?[21] They are suspicious that the story reflects the agenda of the writer of scripture rather than God.

What is Hagar's experience of covenant when viewed through this lens? Phyllis Trible's assessment is a stark one: this story is a "text of terror," a story of triple oppression—based upon nationality, class, and sex.[22] Oh, it's true enough: God *does* honor Hagar as a significant figure. For only God calls her by name, gracing her with the first birth announcement in all of scripture. And, with a covenant similar to Abraham's: "I will so greatly multiply your offspring that they cannot be counted for multitude."[23] But, the patriarchal system takes over. And terror begins.

Hagar's first journey into the wilderness becomes a circle of bondage. According to Trible, Hagar *does* see through the patriarchal system when she becomes pregnant with Abram's child. But, she and Sarai remain stuck there. Sarai uses the power available to her as wife to afflict the Egyptian Hagar, just as the Egyptian Pharaoh will later afflict the Hebrews. And Hagar cannot imagine what freedom looks like. Even God addresses her as "maid of Sarai" and sends her back, to submit to further abuse. But the worst is yet to come: a second and final journey into the wilderness. Exile. God's attentive concern shifted from her to her son. God's covenant with her shifted to Abraham. As God says to Abraham, "As for the son of the slave woman, I will make a nation of him also, because he is your offspring."[24] In the end, Hagar "experiences exodus without liberation, revelation without salvation, wilderness without covenant, wanderings without land, promise without fulfillment, and unmerited exile without return."[25]

The "womanist" Renita Weems basically concurs.[26] The story of Hagar and Sarah "is a story of ethnic prejudice exacerbated by economic and sexual exploitation. Theirs is a story of conflict, women betraying women, mothers conspiring against mothers. Theirs is a story of social rivalry."[27] But she does not let Hagar off the hook. She names Hagar a "passive victim" who "participates in her own exploitation."[28] For Hagar cannot "see" beyond running away; she has no idea where she is going. Is that why, Weems ponders, "the angel had no other choice but to send the runaway slave back to the reality in which she had defined herself"?[29] And yet, the ultimate anguish of the story is this, according to Weems. There is a way in which we are all Hagar's daughters. "When our backs are up against a wall; when we feel abandoned, abused, betrayed, and banished."[30] At times like that, what we most desperately need is a woman to be our sister . . . rather than an abuser.

Finally, it must be noted that other womanists find in Hagar a heroine of survival, one who makes a way where there is no way.[31] And it's true. In the end, she refuses to be passive, seeing to it that Ishmael marries an Egyptian and that her own blood will flow through his descendants.[32]

How can we make our way through this violence done to Hagar? Irmgard Fischer offers us one possible vehicle, by describing the process of writing down the final story, as we are given it. Suspicious of the seeming oppression by God, she holds that the oppressive sections of the story are late additions. She believes that the original story is one of liberation, that the covenant promise to Hagar in Genesis 16:11-12 was the original intention of God. It is a later hand, she believes, that added Genesis 16:9-10, the order to submit and the "carrot" of a multitude of descendants, to the final version of chapter 21. Furthermore, she posits that this material was reworked yet a third time by the priestly writer after the exile.[33] For this priestly writer, Hagar is there only as another wife, to provide Abram with the longed for son of promise (Genesis 16:3). And the covenant with Hagar is really intended for Abram (Genesis 16:15-16), a view that continues into the final reworking of chapter 21. According to Fischer, the priestly writer adds verses 11-13, assuring that Isaac will become the rightful heir of Abraham and that Ishmael will also become father of a nation because he is Abraham's son. In the end, by this final editing, Hagar is left out of the covenant; in the end, it is Abraham's story. In the end, the God of liberation becomes the "God of the Fathers." Even so, we must continue to ask, how can this "God of the Fathers" be measured against the God "who executes justice for the orphan and the widow, and who loves the strangers, providing them food and clothing"?[34]

But there's more. For Phyllis Trible and Renita Weems this story is nothing less than a call to repentance for us today. Hagar lives among us. She is the faithful maid who is exploited, the black woman used and abused by both men and women, the surrogate mother, the resident alien (or refugee) without legal recourse, the other woman, the runaway youth, a pregnant woman alone, the expelled wife, a divorced mother with a child, a homeless woman with a child, or a mother on welfare.[35] And we must "see" her in her full humanity and embrace her.

Some final questions and comments are in order regarding Sarah's experience of the covenant. According to Trible, Sarah is a woman of "privilege and power within the confines of patriarchal structures."[36] Is she wounded herself by that system and unable even to "see" her wound? Has she so absorbed her husband's betrayal of her, twice, that she acts out that pain on another woman? (Remember that Abram/Abraham turned her over twice to another ruler as a wife, so that he would not be harmed.[37] Even though it was part of the culture, what was its effect on Sarah?) In trying to build herself up through Hagar (sharing her husband with Hagar to remove the shame of her barrenness), Sarai is put down, instead . . . by none other than Hagar. What toll did all that take on Sarai? Finally, how could she bear up under the certain knowledge that her own husband would have been willing to kill her only son? Her story ends in anguish, despite the "miraculous" birth of Isaac at God's hand. It is a story that begs for transformation in our day.

## SOME RESOURCES

Fischer, Irmgard, "'Go and Suffer Oppression!' Said God's Messenger to Hagar: Repression of Women in Biblical Texts" In Mary Shawn Copeland and Elisabeth Schüssler Fiorenza, *Violence Against Women*. London: SCM Press, Maryknoll, NY: Orbis Books, 1994, pp. 75-82.

Frankel, Ellen, Ph.D. *The Five Books of Miriam: A Woman's Commentary on the Torah*. San Francisco: Harper, A Division of HarperCollins Publishers, 1998.

Niditch, Susan, "Genesis," as found in Carol A. Newsom and Sharon H. Ringe, editors, *Women's Bible Commentary, Expanded Edition, with Apocrypha*. Louisville, KY: Westminster John Knox Press, 1998.

Nowell, Irene. *Women in the Old Testament*. Collegeville, MN: The Liturgical Press, 1997.

Steinberg, Naomi. *Kinship and Marriage in Genesis: A Household Economics Perspective*. Minneapolis: Fortress Press, 1993.

Syren, Roger. *The Forsaken First-Born: A Study of a Recurrent Motif in the Patriarchal Narratives*. Sheffield, England: Journal for the Study of the Old Testament Press, 1993.

Trible, Phyllis, "Hagar: The Desolation of Rejection" in her *Texts of Terror*. Philadelphia: Fortress Press, 1984.

Weems, Renita J. *Just a Sister Away: A Womanist Vision of Women's Relationships in the Bible*. San Diego, CA: LuraMedia, 1988.

Williams, Dolores. *Sisters in the Wilderness*. Maryknoll, NY: Orbis Books, 1993.

## NOTES

1. See Genesis 11:4.

2. See Genesis 11:8.

3. See Genesis 9:12.

4. See Genesis 12:1.

5. See Genesis 12:2-3.

6. See Genesis 17:17.

7. See Genesis 13:14-16.

8. See Genesis 15:4-5.

9. See Genesis 15:7-21.

10. See Genesis 17:7.

11. See Genesis 17:16. Second Isaiah honors this tradition in Isaiah 51:2 by reminding the people in exile, "Look to Abraham your father and to Sarah who bore you."

12. See Genesis 21:2-5.

13. See Genesis 16.

14. Such affliction is duplicated years later when Pharaoh will afflict the Hebrews in Egypt.

15. She is one of only three women in scripture to be so graced. The other two are the barren wife of Manoah in Judges 13:2-5 and Mary in Luke 1:26-38.

16. See Genesis 21:10.

17. See Genesis 21:12-13.

18. See Genesis 21:14-21.

19. See Genesis 22:1-19; in Genesis 22:2 Isaac is referred to as Abraham's "only son," though truly he is Sarah's only son.

20. It is not just women who are pushed to one side. Robert Syren, in a book entitled *The Forsaken First-Born: A Study of a Recurrent Motif in the Patriarchal Narratives*, explores this theme with regard to Ishmael, Esau, Reuben, and Manasseh. In the case of Ishmael, he concludes that Isaac was given the primary inheritance because of the question about foreign wives after the exile. Like Abraham, true Israelites could not keep foreign wives in their household; however, God did intend that foreigners who converted to Judaism could be accepted into the community.

21. This is known as a hermeneutic (interpretation) of suspicion; Elisabeth Schüssler Fiorenza has written on this at some length.

22. See Phyllis Trible, "Hagar: The Desolation of Rejection," pp. 9-35, in her *Texts of Terror* (Philadelphia: Fortress Press, 1984); hereafter referred to as Trible.

23. See Genesis 16:10.

24. See Genesis 21:13.

25. Trible, p. 28.

26. A womanist is a black feminist. The word comes from novelist Alice Walker and describes a courageous woman who is committed to making people whole, men and women alike.

27. Renita J. Weems, "A Mistress, A Maid, and No Mercy," p. 2, in her *Just a Sister Away* (San Diego: LuraMedia, 1988); hereafter referred to as Weems.

28. Weems, p. 12.

29. Weems, p. 13.

30. Weems, p. 17.

31. See, for example, Dolores Williams, *Sisters in the Wilderness* (Maryknoll, NY: Orbis Books, 1993).

32. See Genesis 21:21.

33. The priestly writer was named early in the twentieth century. Scripture scholars in the previous two centuries had increasingly questioned the traditional notion that Moses was the writer of the Torah (first five books of the Hebrew scripture: Genesis, Exodus, Leviticus, Numbers, Deuteronomy). They noticed the differences in style, content, and storytelling that are found in these books.

    Out of this questioning emerged a thesis by Julius Wellhausen (who died in 1918), which scholars today accept with a few modifications. It is acknowledged that there are four "traditions," oral and written, which make up the Torah: 1) the J or Yahwist, dating from the tenth and ninth centuries B.C.E., 2) the E or Elohist, from the same time period, 3) the D or Deuteronomic, from the seventh century B.C.E. (post-exilic period), 4) the P or Priestly tradition.

    Generally, the purpose of the priestly writer (or tradition) is to provide a foundation for the true worship of God to people who have been scattered to the four winds. The cult is important, as is the genealogy of the generations (*toledot*), including God's promises to the patriarchs. In Genesis, the priestly writer shows up at the very beginning (1:1–2:3) in the systematic ordering of creation. (Note, for example, that Sabbath rest is based upon God's resting at the dawn of creation.) Also, the priestly writer works with the stories of promise to add material that roots the Jewish people in the patriarchs. (See, for example, the recognized priestly insertions of 16:1a, 3, and 15-16 and 21:1b-5 into Hagar's story.)

34. See Deuteronomy 10:18.

35. Trible, p. 28.

36. Trible, p. 9.

37. See Genesis 12:10-20 and Genesis 20.

# four

THE PERSISTENT WIDOW

# We Cry Out for Justice as We Persevere

The story of the persistent widow and the unjust judge (Luke 18:1-8) appears in the Roman Catholic Lectionary on the 29th Sunday in Ordinary Time, Cycle C. It is paired with a story that reveals God's prayer in action, the prayer of Moses and others that allows Israel to prevail against Amalek. Luke has placed the parable within the context of prayer. True prayer is a continual call to repent, to turn so as to see our one true God. True prayer opens the heart to do justice, as the second reading in this worship service so clearly expresses. True prayer moves the heart and the voice to break silence in the face of oppression. True prayer is intimately connected to action on God's behalf; and true action on God's behalf can come only out of prayer. It is the widow in this parable who shows us the working of prayer in the human heart.

While this story does not appear in the Lenten readings, it might well be celebrated at that time of the year. It is a story of conversion for everyone. It is a story of doing justice in God's eyes. It is a story that reveals our limits, but most especially God's ever-faithful love for each and every one of us.

With this in mind, the gathering space is sparse, with decor that would remind participants of the need for ongoing change of heart. The same is true of the worship space itself. In the very center of the seating area is a bare table with a bowl of ashes on it. A simple wooden cross might also be a visible part of the worship area; or the cross might welcome people in the gathering space. If this service is celebrated in the evening, there might be candlelight throughout the worship area.

*Ministers:* leader, widow, one or two readers, cantor, and musicians

*Materials:* table, bowl of ashes

## Introductory Rites

### CALL TO WORSHIP                                    *Please stand*

Leader:    God's Spirit stirs in our hearts.

All:       Cry out with God for justice!

Leader:    God's Spirit stirs in our hearts.

All:       Break the bonds of silence,
           let the oppressed go free!

Leader:    God's Spirit stirs in our hearts.

All:       For God waits . . . in women crying out,
           in children abandoned . . . and in anyone kept at bay.

Leader:    God's Spirit stirs in our hearts.

All:       For when we keep anyone on the margins,
           we rob God . . . and ourselves, of God's power in our midst.

Leader:    God's Spirit stirs in our hearts.

All:       That our prayer may become action for God. Amen.

### GATHERING HYMN

"Song of St. Patrick," text by Marty Haugen, based on "St. Patrick's Breastplate," tune by Marty Haugen, GIA Publications, Inc., © 1986.

## Liturgy of the Word

### DEUTERONOMY 10:12-13, 17-18 *(Reader)*          *Please be seated*

PSALM 68
. . . . . . .

"You Have Made a Home for the Poor," text by Rory Cooney (based on Psalm 68:4-5, 6-7, 10-11), tune by Rory Cooney, GIA Publications, Inc., © 1991.


ROMANS 8:22-28 *(Reader)*
. . . . . . . . . . . . . . . . . .

GOSPEL ACCLAMATION:
*Lenten acclamation (if during Lent) or Alleluia*
. . . . . . . . . . . . . . . . . . . . . . . . . . . . .

LUKE 18:1-8 *(Leader and Widow)*
. . . . . . . . . . . . . . . . . . . . . . . . .

*Leader introduces the widow.*

Life is often not what it seems. And God is sometimes found in the people, places, and situations we least expect. Even in a seemingly dependent widow with nothing to offer. Listen well, as she tells her story.

*Widow's reflection.*

Walk with me, won't you? I'm on my way to the judge's house. To knock on his door, once again. And demand justice from him, once again. You see, not long ago my husband died. And we had no children, so all his inheritance comes to me. But my brother-in-law, instead of taking my side, as the Torah says he should, wants a good chunk of the money for himself. And that simply isn't right! What will happen to me? He has enough, as it is, but I could end up with nothing, as soon as the little bit he says I should receive runs out.

Some people are really upset with me, I don't mind telling you. They say I should keep quiet and stay in my place. After all, they tell me, it's up to the men to argue for justice, especially in front of a judge. And, they say I should never go to the judge's house, even though my opponent has already done precisely that. Yes, I'm sure of it—my brother-in-law has offered the judge a bribe in order to win the case.

Are you upset with me, too? Or can you possibly understand how it is for me? There's something inside me—deep within—that will *not* let me keep silent in the face of injustice. I *must* speak out; I *must* break the silence. After all, I know God. I know the God who set our people free, the God who gave us the Torah so that we might treat one another with dignity and respect. And, I know our prayers to God, our psalms. There are two that have been going through my heart and mind, over and over, ever since my husband died.

> Bless the Lord, O my soul,
> and do not forget all his benefits,
> who forgives all your iniquity,
> who heals all your diseases,
> who redeems your life from the pit,
> who crowns you with steadfast love and mercy. . . .
> The Lord works vindication and justice
> for all who are oppressed.[1]

And, more recently,

> Father of orphans and protector of widows
> is God in his holy habitation.
> God gives the desolate a home to live in."[2]

Now I believe that God intends our prayer to be put into action. Certainly God expects judges to rule fairly and to render verdicts on behalf of those who have little, like myself. And, if judges need a nudge to do it, well, sometimes that's where prayer takes us.

Of course, here's where I need to be careful. Whenever I'm so passionate for justice, like I am right now, I could tip over the edge into revenge. Do you know what I mean? I'm not out to hurt my brother-in-law *or* the judge, though people tell me the judge is accusing *me* of badgering *him*, of literally making him black and blue from my verbal assaults for justice. It's simply this: I know that the system is not working as God intends. I know of scribal retainers who interpret the Torah to suit those who are rich and take away from those who are poor. I know of judges who make decisions based on this inequality, especially if someone has just lined their pockets with a little money. I know that this injustice has to stop. So, not only do I have to keep coming back to the judge, I have to keep coming back to God. I have to keep praying to God that I might stay focused on setting things right without hurting anyone in the process. That's no easy task, I will tell you. But that's how it must be. Maybe you can understand, from some of the struggles in your life.

Walk with me, won't you, on the path of justice.

*Silence*

## MUSICAL REFLECTION

"Abundant Life," text by Ruth Duck, GIA Publications, Inc., © 1992, tune: "La Grange," adapted by Marty Haugen, GIA Publications, Inc., © 1994.

# Ritual of Conversion (with ashes)

## INTRODUCTION (Leader)

Ashes are a sign of our need for God. The widow in us needs strength and openness of heart to remain true to the God within. The judge in us needs to return to God's way of seeing things. The opponent in us needs to see where we have gone astray by wounding others. Each of us, at one time or another, needs to repent: to turn and begin again, to turn and see the mercy of our ever faithful God. Ashes are a sign of God's reign in our midst, the assurance that new life can emerge from every turning away, every weakness, every death, and every failure. When you are ready for ashes, then, please come forward.

## SIGNING WITH ASHES

*Leader, widow, and readers sign one another with ashes; then the leader and the widow invite each participant to come forward for ashes. Everyone will hear the same words, which the leaders have offered to each other: "Repent, turn and see the face of God, and proclaim God's reign of justice."*

## MUSIC DURING THE RITUAL

"Ashes," text and tune by Tom Conry, New Dawn Music, © 1978.

or

"Healer of Our Every Ill," text and tune by Marty Haugen, GIA Publications, Inc., © 1987.

## LITANY

Leader:     From peace that is no peace,

All:        deliver us, O God.

Leader:     From righteousness that is narrow-minded and violent,

All:        deliver us, O God.

Leader:     From blindness and deafness to the needs of those around us,

All:        deliver us, O God.

Leader:     From hardness of heart to our own need for change,

All:        deliver us, O God.

Leader:     From silence in the face of injustice,

All:        deliver us, O God.

Leader:     From good intentions paralyzed by inaction,

All:        deliver us, O God.

Leader:     From complicity with systems that wound people,

All:        deliver us, O God.


Leader:     For the will to examine our hearts and our systems,

All:        prepare us, O God.

Leader:     For eyes to see you and ears to hear you,

            in common and uncommon places,

All:        prepare us, O God.

Leader:     For a heart that is vulnerable to the needs of your people,

All:        prepare us, O God.

Leader:     For the energy to do something about those needs,

All:        prepare us, O God.

Leader:     For the spark to set the earth on fire for justice,

All:        prepare us, O God.

Leader:     For the integrity to only enkindle a holy blaze,

All:        prepare us, O God.

Leader:     For the persistence to bring about your reign, in the her and now,

All:        prepare us, O God.

THE LORD'S PRAYER *(slowly and reflectively)*                *Please stand*

## Closing Rites

### BLESSING

*Leader invites each "half" to face the other, extend an arm in blessing, and together bless one another, as follows:*

To the extent that you have been hungry,
go forth with God's hunger for justice.
To the extent that you have been thirsty,
go forth with God's thirst to comfort the afflicted
and make a home for the alienated.
To the extent that you have known love,
go forth, that Love might infuse and fortify your hunger and thirst.
Go forth with the Creator's vision,
go forth with the dreams of Jesus,
go forth with the Spirit of Christ
to build the reign of God on the earth.

### CLOSING HYMN

"Canticle of the Turning," text by Rory Cooney (based on Luke 1:46-58), tune, "Star of the County Down," Irish traditional, arr. by Rory Cooney, GIA Publications, Inc., © 1990.

### NOTES

1.    Psalm 103:3-4, 6.

2.    Psalm 68:5-6a.

## The Persistent Widow of Luke 18:1-8

Imagine the face of God. Imagine the face of persistent longing for justice that refuses to take no for an answer. Meet the persistent widow of Luke's Gospel: image of God, prowling the earth for justice, like a lioness out to protect her children; image of the Wisdom Woman crying out at the city gates, offering a treasury of truth and good advice, of strength and insight;[1] image of renewed humanity, striving to set things right with the world.

## THE CONTEXT OF THE PARABLE IN LUKE'S GOSPEL

A parable turns things upside down. A parable takes what is familiar and adds a twist . . . to disturb the comfortable and give assurance to the downtrodden. A parable is capable of being interpreted in a variety of ways.

The Lucan Jesus tells a story of a widow and a judge; each figure is familiar to his audience, with a familiar set of expectations. But the story has a few surprises. And Luke adds to the mix by inserting this little story within the context of prayer. In effect, he says that this story is to be taken seriously. For the Lucan Jesus is at prayer during most of his significant "red letter" days: his baptism (Luke 3:21-22), his selection of the twelve (Luke 6:12-16), Peter's confession of Jesus as the "Messiah of God" (Luke 9:28-36), Jesus' instruction of his disciples in prayer (Luke 11:1-4), his prayer of anguish at the Mount of Olives on the night before his Passion (Luke 22:39-46), and his final handing over of his spirit to his Father (Luke 23:46). If prayer was so essential to Jesus, how much more necessary was it to his disciples of the eighties, when Luke was writing this gospel. For he saw a church under continual threat of persecution, struggling to remain faithful to Jesus during the indefinite delay of his Second Coming. It is in that context that Luke tells this little story.

## THE PARABLE ITSELF

Most scholars now agree that the parable itself is contained in 18:2-5, although Joseph Fitzmyer would add verse 6, in order to return to the attitude of the judge.[2] Everyone who first heard the parable knew what to expect of a judge and a widow. A judge was to take the place of God among the people in rendering verdicts, for God judges "the people with equity and [guides] the nations upon earth."[3] Indeed, the God of Israel is the one who "is not partial and takes no bribe, who executes justice for the orphan and the widow, the strangers, providing them food and clothing."[4] And all the people of Israel were expected to respond as generously to the stranger themselves, for they had once been "strangers in the land of Egypt."[5] Love that had freed the people from slavery demanded it.[6] And Wisdom teaching insisted that everyone "give to the

Most High as he has given to you, and as generously as you can afford."[7] Indeed, the prayer of such a just person "pierces the clouds," not resting "until it reaches its goal."[8] God will not delay in answering such prayer, so that all can rejoice in God's mercy.[9] At the same time, a judge held special responsibility in this covenant relationship. King Jehoshaphat of Judah had put the matter well, in challenging his newly appointed judges, "Consider what you are doing, for you judge not on behalf of human beings but on the Lord's behalf; he is with you in giving judgement. Now, let the fear of the Lord be upon you; take care what you do, for there is no perversion of justice with the Lord our God, or partiality, or taking of bribes."[10]

Everyone understood about widows, as well. It was a man's world, and a woman was generally dependent on a man for sustenance and justice. Most often she went from her father's house to her husband's house. But a widow was most vulnerable of all. In some effort to provide a buffer against destitution for a widow—and to provide an heir for her dead husband—the custom of levirate marriage was written into law.[11] This meant that the brother of the dead man was to take her in marriage and produce an heir for his dead brother, assuring that the dead man's name would not be blotted out of tribal memory. The familiar stories of the widowed Tamar—who persistently plotted for an heir from Judah[12]—and the widowed Ruth—who married Boaz only after the next of kin expressed no interest in her[13]—reflected this practice. But, what if the widow had no brother-in-law? Who would care for her then? If she were fortunate enough to have a son, "the first-born son was required by law to care for her until he was thirty years old."[14] These options provided the basis for her rights.

The expectation is, then, that the widow is dependent on the judge for what is right, and that he will act honorably. But that is not what happens. The judge is totally corrupt, a man of wickedness, in fact, as Wisdom judges human behavior. And the widow, knowing her rights, chooses to take action in a way that is anything but helpless and dependent. Oh, she knows she must seek justice from the judge, but she refuses to leave him alone until her opponent (son? brother-in-law?) is made to follow the law.

## AN INTERPRETATION OF THE PARABLE

What did Jesus intend in the telling of this story? What did Luke intend in placing this parable within the context of prayer? How might we all be challenged by this story today?

We simply don't know what Jesus had in mind. So, turning to Luke, interpreters have generally taken him seriously about his emphasis on prayer. The usual interpretation has gone something like this, with the argument from lesser to greater. If a corrupt judge can respond to a person in need and give her what she rightly seeks, regardless of his intention, how much more will God respond—surely and swiftly—to the prayer of God's chosen ones. Such an interpretation retains the judge as the God figure but makes the obvious distinction between God and *this* judge.

And yet, such an interpretation has caused uneasiness, consistently raising some disturbing questions. Are we being told to "badger" God in prayer? Is it suggested that God will respond to the prayer of anyone who is just? What if God does not seem to respond? What, exactly, *is* prayer? And, how is it related to doing justice? Where *is* God to be found in this story?

Perhaps another "take" on the story will open up some sound theological approaches to these questions. In what follows, I borrow from the work of William Herzog, one of several contemporary scripture scholars who penetrates the political, economic, and social scene of Jesus' day.[15] In his commentary, entitled "Justice at the Gate?" Herzog paints a picture of a corrupt system. The ideal Torah was one thing. But an informal, oral Torah had also developed, to serve the interests of the ruling elite, rather than the downtrodden.[16] It was common enough for scribal retainers to re-codify the Torah in favor of the rich. And judges could always be found who would make decisions in line with this informal "Torah." All that was necessary was a bribe from the right party.

For Herzog, this judge fits the bill. He is rendering the verdict himself, rather than as part of the prescribed tribunal of three or seven. After all, bribes are more effective this way. He is probably operating out of a small city (a market or administrative center) or a larger center like Jerusalem or Tiberius. And the case most likely has to do with this widow's inheritance rights. As a widow, she is entitled to live off her husband's estate, unless she returns to her father's house.[17] She might also press a claim to levirate marriage with an unmarried brother; and this might cause tension in the household if he wanted no part of it. In any case, her inheritance is probably a sizable sum, enough to create such a stir. And, *she* is regarded as property to be transferred and settled, so that household arrangements might become stable, once again.[18] Summarizing the system, Herzog says this: "When one descends from the rarefied atmosphere of the ideals into the details of everyday life, the

Drawing From Wisdom's Well

Torah changes. It becomes a tool for legitimization and social control, prescribing and proscribing behavior, and it is also employed to protect the interest of a ruling class."[19]

Enter the widow. Notice that she goes before the judge herself, a startling thing, for it is a breach of etiquette.[20] But she knows her rights, and she knows the system. She knows that her opponent (probably a family member) is working behind the scenes to influence the decision. So she does the same thing, going to the judge, again and again, demanding vindication, calling the judge to accountability. She breaks the silence, naming the "domination system"[21] for what it is. "When anyone steps out of the system and tells the truth, lives the truth, that enables everyone else to peer behind the curtain too."[22] Returning to Herzog's title of his commentary, she is reminiscent of the Wisdom Woman of Proverbs, crying out at the city gates for people to follow her path of justice.

Both Megan McKenna and Barbara Reid have taken the next step, suggesting that this widow is none other than an image of God. *She* is where God is found, not in the judge. Certainly, the prophets proclaim that God is to be found in the cries of the poor, especially in their clamors for justice. And, Christians believe in a God who became vulnerable for us, taking on the weakness of human flesh. In this parable, justice is birthed out of the apparent weakness of a widow; in the Mystery of God, new life emerges out of the apparent weakness of a love that is willing to go to the Cross for us. Barbara Reid believes that Jesus intended to shatter all stereotypes in telling this story, that he meant for us to see God in the widow. But, she says, Luke resists the implications of identifying God with the widow by naming her as the persistent intercessor.[23] This may well be true, for feminists have documented Luke's "silencing" of women in the Acts of the Apostles.[24] And yet, as Paul assures us, the Spirit of God prays in and through us, interceding on our behalf when we do not know how to pray, moving us to action for justice.[25] If the widow embodies the prayer of God, could Luke possibly be suggesting that God is truly to be found in this woman, praying and acting for justice? If so, it would certainly accord with one of Luke's favorite themes, the upside-down nature of our God, whose "mercy is for those who fear him," . . . who "has scattered the proud . . . and sent the rich away empty."[26] What do you think?

## SOME RESOURCES

. . . . . . . . . . . . .

Fitzmyer, Joseph A., S.J. *The Anchor Bible: The Gospel According to Luke (X-XXIV)*. Garden City, NY: Doubleday & Company, Inc., 1985.

Herzog, William R. II. *Parables as Subversive Speech: Jesus as Pedagogue of the Oppressed*. Louisville, KY: Westminster John Knox Press, 1994.

McKenna, Megan. *Parables: The Arrows of God*. Maryknoll, NY: Orbis Press, 1994.

Praeder, Susan Marie. *The Word in Women's Worlds*. Wilmington, DE: Michael Glazier, 1988.

Reid, Barbara E. *Choosing the Better Part?: Women in the Gospel of Luke*. Collegeville, MN: The Liturgical Press. A Michael Glazier Book, 1996.

Scott, Bernard Brandon. *Hear Then the Parable: A Commentary on the Parables of Jesus*. Minneapolis: Fortress Press, 1989.

## NOTES

● ● ● ● ●

1. See Proverbs 8:1-21.

2. Joseph A. Fitzmyer, S.J. *The Anchor Bible: The Gospel According to Luke (X-XXIV)* (Garden City, NY: Doubleday & Company, Inc., 1985), p. 1176.

3. Psalm 67:4.

4. Deuteronomy 10:17-18. See also Sirach 35:15-25.

5. Deuteronomy 10:19.

6. See the command in Leviticus 19:33-34.

7. Sirach 35:12.

8. Sirach 35:21.

9. Sirach 35:22-25.

10. 2 Chronicles 19:6-7.

11. See Deuteronomy 25:5-10.

12. See Genesis, chapter 38.

13. See Ruth 4:7-12.

14. Megan McKenna, *Parables: The Arrows of God* (Maryknoll, NY: Orbis Press, 1994), p. 107. She bases this on some Jewish commentaries of the law.

15. William R. Herzog II, *Parables as Subversive Speech: Jesus as Pedagogue of the Oppressed* (Louisville, KY: Westminster John Knox Press, 1994); hereafter referred to as Herzog.

16. Herzog, pp. 224-25.

17. Herzog, p. 223.

18. Ibid.

19. Herzog, p. 228.

20. Ibid.

21. This is a term used by Walter Wink in his book *Engaging the Powers* (Minneapolis: Fortress Press, 1992) to describe an unjust system or structure of control; hereafter referred to as Wink.

22. Wink, p. 98.

23. Barbara E. Reid, *Choosing the Better Part?: Women in the Gospel of Luke* (Collegeville, MN: The Liturgical Press, 1996), p. 194.

24. See, for example, Gail R. O'Day, "Acts," in *Women's Bible Commentary, Expanded Edition with Apocrypha* (Louisville, KY: Westminster John Knox Press, 1998), ed. Carol A. Newsom and Sharon H. Ringe. On p. 395 she says, "Luke's desire to present a picture of Christianity that would win favor in the Roman Empire led to a further diminishment of women's roles in Acts."

25. See Romans 8:26-27.

26. See Luke 1:50, 51, 53. This is taken from the "Magnificat" of Mary.

*five*

THE DAUGHTERS OF "Z"

# We Stand Between Promise and Fulfillment

*The baptismal font (or a large bowl of water taken from the font and placed upon a table) and Easter candle are the main focus. Some green plants are near the water, as well. Musicians are to one side and the leader and commentator are on the other side. Storytellers will come up from the assembly.*

Ministers:   *leader, commentator, storytellers, cantor, musicians, and liturgical dancers*

Materials:   *table with a bowl of water or the baptismal font, Easter candle, green plants, streamers*

*As the assembly gathers, the choir sings:* "Before the World Began," text by John L. Bell to the tune "Incarnation," text and music © 1987, arrangement © 1995, Wild Goose Resource Group, the Iona Community, from the collection *God Never Sleeps*, GIA Publications, Inc. *This is a gentle hymn which proclaims God's sure promise, that "I am for you."*

Rehearsal of the Opening Hymn, "Come All You People." *This is a joyful hymn in response to God's promise; it is also a hymn that is easy to learn, providing a good gathering exercise. It sets the tone that God's Jubilee is for everyone.*

# Introductory Rites

## OPENING HYMN

*Please stand*

"Come All You People," tune and words by Alexander Gondo, arrangement by John L. Bell, The Iona Community, GIA Publications, Inc., © 1994. *Liturgical dancers with brightly colored streamers come in, leading the storytellers, one of whom carries the Book, and the commentator and leader.*

## OPENING PRAYER

Leader:   Let us pray.
Gather all your people, O God of the universe,
gather us in, from every corner of time and space.

All:   Sound the trumpet!
Announce Jubilee!
Call forth the spirit of our ancestors,
and mingle their breath with our own,
so that *all* your children might welcome this great day.

Leader:   Unroll the scroll of your righteousness and peace
and speak to us of your mercy.
Disturb us with your dreams,
so that kindness and truth might embrace.

All:   This we ask,
in the name of Jesus, the Christ,
whose name is sealed upon our hearts forever. Amen!

# Liturgy of the Word

*Please be seated*

### A STORY OF PROMISE: THE STORY OF MAHLAH, NOAH, HOGLAH, MILCAH, AND TIRZAH
*(told by one of the storytellers)*

Once upon a long time ago, as the people of Israel were preparing to enter into the Promised Land, there was excitement in the air. At campfires in the evening, the men would gather, making plans for the land they would inherit. But in one camp, there was no excitement. There was no rejoicing. Mahlah, Noah, Hoglah, Milcah, and Tirzah, commonly known as the daughters of "Z"—or the daughters of Zelophehad—were disturbed. Deeply troubled. Their father had remained faithful to Yahweh all these many years of wandering, but he had died out in the wilderness. There would *be* no land for him. Indeed, *his* name might be lost forever from his tribe of Manasseh, son of Joseph.

What would they do? What *could* they do? At night, around their camp-fire, their conversation went something like this. "Moses is dividing the land among the men. Our father is dead, and we have no brothers. The law says that only sons shall inherit. We *must* do something or there will be no land for *us*."[1] "Yes," another agreed. "If it were our enemies who were keeping us from the land, we could understand, but it is our very own people. For years we have put up with each other. Together we have endured the sharp bristles of the cactus, the sting of the scorpions and the spitting of the camels."[2] And they all agreed, "We must act before it is too late or our hope and our father's memory will die away with this fire."[3] "We will have nothing and our children's children will have nothing."

Finally, one said, "I know what we'll do! You remember Miriam, and how she sang and danced and led us in prayer . . . not only at the Red Sea, but whenever we needed courage. She died out in the wilderness, too, but she would advocate for us now, if she were here. So, tomorrow we will go before Moses and the judges and tell them that they *must* give us a share of the land that is allotted to the tribe of Manasseh, son of Joseph." All the sisters agreed.

And so, the very next day, they "stood before Moses, Eleazar the priest, the leaders, and all the congregation, at the entrance of the tent of meeting."[4] They pleaded their case . . . and there was a great silence. Then Moses finally spoke, "Mahlah, Noah, Hoglah, Milcah, and Tirzah, I cannot decide. I must take your case to God." So, while Moses spoke with God, the five daughters prayed the prayers of their people to the God of their ancestors. God spoke to Moses and said, "Zelophehad's daughters are right in what they are saying; you shall indeed let them possess an inheritance among their father's brothers and pass the inheritance of their father on to them. You shall also say to the Israelites, 'If a man dies, and has no son, then you shall pass his inheritance on to his daughter.'"[5]

And it was so. But some of the men grumbled. "What will happen when the daughters marry outside our tribe? They will take their land with them. How will that be fair?" And so it was that the men of the tribe of Manasseh convinced Moses to make one more law, requiring daughters who inherited land to marry within their tribe. The daughters of "Z" were sad, and so was God.[6] But one spoke for all, as she held on to the promise of God, "One day, my sisters, the law will change, and we will receive the full gift of our inheritance with all its freedom and all its responsibilities. Until then, we *must* keep alive and pass on the certain knowledge that God's love is for us *all*."

## MUSICAL RESPONSE
• • • • • • • • • • • • • • •

"Freedom Is Coming," a South African freedom song, collected by Anders Nyberg, arr. by Henry H. Leck, Utryck © 1984, this arrangement found in *God Never Sleeps, Songs from the Iona Community*, GIA Publications, Inc., Utryck © 1994. *The musicians begin this refrain, which is easy to "pick up." Everyone is invited to sing the refrain several times.*

## COMMENTATOR
• • • • • • • • • • • •

In the fullness of time, The Word of God, the Child and Prophet of Wisdom, became Holy Ground. Jesus grew in age and wisdom . . . taught . . . told stories . . . healed . . . transformed lives . . . called disciples and formed community . . . spoke God's truth . . . and revealed the God who is with us and for us. One day in his ministry went like this:

## A STORY OF DELIVERANCE
• • • • • • • • • • • • • • • • • • • • • • • •

*The Story of the Bent Over Woman (Luke 13:10-17), memorized and told as a story by the other storyteller.*

Now Jesus was teaching in one of the synagogues on the Sabbath. And just then there appeared a woman with a spirit that had crippled her for eighteen years. She was bent over and was quite unable to stand up straight. When Jesus saw her, he called her over and said, "Woman, you are set free from your ailment." When he laid his hands on her, immediately she stood up straight and began praising God. But the leader of the synagogue, indignant because Jesus had cured on the Sabbath, kept saying to the crowd, "There are six days on which work ought to be done; come on those days and be cured, and not on the Sabbath day." But the Lord answered him and said, "You hypocrites! Does not each of you on the Sabbath untie his ox or his donkey from the manger, and lead it away to give it water? And ought not this woman, a daughter of Abraham whom Satan bound for eighteen long years, be set free from this bondage on the Sabbath day?" When he said this, all his opponents were put to shame; and the entire crowd was rejoicing at all the wonderful things that he was doing.

## COMMENTATOR
• • • • • • • • • • • •

What had kept this woman bent over for eighteen *very* long years? Was it a physical ailment only, something for which the doctors of her day would have no name and no cure? Something like osteoporosis? Or was she bent over from deep within? Was there something in this woman that longed to praise God in the synagogue, in the space that the men had reserved for themselves? We don't know, of course. But we do know this. After all this time, there she was, lingering on the margins of official prayer, waiting. . . . And we also know this! Jesus dared to see with the heart of God. He called her forth, front and center, into that previously all-male space. And then he restored this woman's inheritance, the land of her very own body. He named her a daughter of Abraham, inheritor of God's promises, the only woman so-named in all of scripture. He dared to imagine beyond rule-bound confines, that we might do the same.

## MUSICAL RESPONSE
• • • • • • • • • • • • • •

"If You Believe and I Believe," text is a Zimbabwean traditional, music is a Zimbabwean derivative of English folk melody, arranged by John L. Bell, in the collection, *God Never Sleeps*. Arrangement Wild Goose Resource Group, The Iona Community, GIA Publications, Inc., © 1991.

# Response to the Word: Ritual of Inheritance
• • • • • • • • • • • • • • • • • • • • • • • • • • • • • • • • • • • • • • • • • •

## INVITATION TO THE RITUAL *(Leader)*
• • • • • • • • • • • • • • • • • • • • • • • • • • •

Through our baptism, God has given us the land . . . the land of our very own bodies, as part of the Body of Christ. It is both gift and responsibility. To offer recovery of sight to the blind. Release for the captives and a year of favor from our God. It is a land that must be worked in right relationship. A land that needs to be fertilized with healing, hope, and forgiveness, seventy times seven. A land where nobody gets left out. A land that needs space for grace, that requires Sabbath rest and refreshment . . . so that it might produce good fruit, a harvest of justice.

Can you dare to imagine such a land? The land of the Body of Christ as God sees it? A land where nobody is bent over from too little food . . . health care . . . housing . . . education and the like . . . where nobody is withered up and bent double because their church or society *refuses* to welcome their God-given gifts, so freely offered.

If you can imagine being part of such Holy Ground, I invite you to respond "I do" to the following vision:[7]

Leader:     Do you dare to "re-imagine what it means to be a full human being made in the image of God, and to live and speak this truth in our daily lives"?

Response:  I do.

Leader:     Do you dare to "re-imagine what it means to be the whole body of Christ"?

Response:  I do.

Leader:     Do you dare to pattern your life on biblical justice, "which mandates that all persons share in right relationship with each other, with the cosmos, and with the Creator"?

Response:  I do.

I now invite you to seal your commitment to this harvest of justice with the waters of baptism. Please come forward, as you wish, touch the water, and declare your commitment to one of the leaders. Be as specific as possible. For example:

- "I commit myself to a better world for children."

- "I commit myself to a compassionate world for our aging population."

- "I commit myself to full and equal partnership in our church."

- "I commit myself to restorative justice rather than punishment."

- "I commit myself to _____ (whatever is your passion)."

If you cannot be specific, you might say, "I commit myself to working for the world that God envisions."

## MUSIC DURING THE RITUAL

"Song Over the Waters," text and tune by Marty Haugen, GIA Publications, Inc., © 1987. *If needed, continue with* "Healing River," text by Fran Minkoff, tune by Fred Hellerman, arr. by Michael Joncas, Appleseed Music, Inc., © 1964.

# Closing Rites

## SENDING FORTH BLESSING *(Leader and all)* *Please stand*

May our bodies, Christ's body, be blest:
our eyes for piercing the darkness of doubt,
our ears for tending to the cries of the wounded,
our arms for embracing the leper . . . and the lonely,
our hands for holding the vulnerable . . . and the strong,
our feet for standing firm in the harvest of justice,
our hearts for passion and compassion,
our wills conformed to that of our Maker,
through the furnace of just anger and molten love
for the honor and glory of God,
always and forever. Amen!

## CONCLUDING HYMN

"Awake, O Sleeper," text by Marty Haugen (based on Ephesians 50), tune by Marty Haugen, GIA Publications, Inc., © 1987.

or

"On Holy Ground," text and tune by Donna Pena, acc. by Diana Kodner, GIA Publications, Inc., © 1992, 1994.

## NOTES

1. Rabbi Sandy Eisenberg Sasso, "The Daughters of Z" in *But God Remembered* (Woodstock, VT: Jewish Lights Publishing, 1995), p. 26; hereafter referred to as Sasso.

2. Ibid.

3. Ibid.

4.   Book of Numbers 27:2; the story of these five daughters is told in Numbers 27:1-11 and 36:1-12.

5.   Book of Numbers 27:7-8.

6.   Sasso, p. 29.

7.   This is taken from the Madaleva Manifesto, signed on April 29, 2000, on the Feast of Catherine of Siena, at St. Mary's College, Notre Dame, Indiana, by sixteen American women, highly respected theologians in the "catholic tradition," lecturers in the Madaleva series. They are Sr. Mary C. Boys, Lisa Sowle Cahill, Denise L. Carmody, Benedictine Srs. Joan Chittister and Mary Collins, Elizabeth A. Dreyer, Maria Harris, Monika K. Hellwig, Dominican Sr. Mary Catherine Hilkert, Sister of St. Joseph Elizabeth A. Johnson, Dolores R. Leckey, Gail Porter Mandel, Kathleen Norris, Jeanette Rodriguez, Immaculate Heart of Mary Sr. Sandra M. Schneiders.

# The Story of Mahlah, Noah, Hoglah, Milcah, and Tirzah, Otherwise Known as the Daughters of "Z," or the Daughters of Zelophehad

## (Numbers 27:1-11 and 36:1-12)

This story of Mahlah, Noah, Hoglah, Milcah, and Tirzah is a gem. And it is an unknown gem, even to many who are otherwise familiar with scripture. It is the story of inheritance, the story of five courageous women, who not only confront the judges and elders of their people, but their leader Moses, and even God, who has just ruled on how the Promised Land is to be divided up among the tribes (see Numbers 26:52-56).

The events in this story take place at the conclusion of forty wearisome years of Israelite wandering in the wilderness, just as the people are about to cross over into the Promised Land. A second census has just been taken, as directed by God, and God has just given instructions to Moses about the division of that land. Provision is made only for the men, as is the custom. But that is not good enough for these five daughters. They plead their cause at the entrance of the tent of meeting, confident that their God "is good to all, and his compassion is over all that he has made" (Psalm 145:9). As they proclaim so passionately, "Our father died in the wilderness; . . . and he had no sons. Why should the name of our father be taken away from his clan because he had no son? Give to us a possession among our father's brothers" (Numbers 27:3a, 4).

Moses had no answer . . . so he brought the case to God. And it was God who declared, "The daughters of Zelophehad are right in what they are saying" (Numbers 27:7a). However, this is not the end of the story. The men of their tribe, the tribe of Manasseh, son of Joseph, murmur and grumble. "If they are married into another Israelite tribe, then their inheritance will be taken from the inheritance of our ancestors and added to the inheritance of the tribe into which they marry" (Numbers 36:3). This time Moses does not consult God and simply makes one more law. Women who inherit land can "marry whom they think best; only it must be into a clan of their father's tribe that they are married, so that no inheritance of the Israelites shall be transferred from one tribe to another" (Numbers 36:6b-7a). And so it was that there was a beginning of women's inheritance.

There are many differences of opinion on the importance of this story. The rabbis teach that these five daughters are "so wise, pious, and learned" that "they choose to remain unmarried for forty years because they cannot find suitable partners. As a result of their piety, when they later marry, they all miraculously give birth at 130, like Moses' mother, Yokheved."[1] Some Jewish sages today suggest that "this story justifies why women were later permitted to inherit land within a patriarchal system."[2] Still others hold that the Jewish law is flexible enough to embrace women, extending the common Jewish legacy to them, as well as to men.[3] One scholar asks: why is this story retained in the scripture? She concludes that it does have to do with the land and that it provides comfort for men as well as for women. Women are in a better, though limited place, at the conclusion of this story, knowing that there is some vehicle for inheriting the land. And men are assured that their names will not be cut off from their clans.[4]

## SOME RESOURCES
. . . . . . . . . . . . . . .

Frankel, Ellen, Ph.D. *The Five Books of Miriam*. San Francisco: Harper, 1998.

Sakenfeld, Katharine Doob, "In the Wilderness, Awaiting the Land: The Daughters of Zelophehad and Feminist Interpretation." *Theology Today* 46 (1989), pp. 154-168.

_____. "Numbers," as found in *Women's Bible Commentary*, Ed. Carol A. Newsom and Sharon H. Ringe. Louisville: Westminster John Knox Press, 1998, pp. 49-56.

Sasso, Rabbi Sandy Eisenberg. "The Daughters of Z," in her *But God Remembered: Stories of Women From Creation to the Promised Land*. Woodstock, VT: Jewish Lights Publishing, 1995.

## NOTES

• • • • •

1. Ellen Frankel, Ph.D., *The Five Books of Miriam* (San Francisco: Harper), 1998, p. 235.

2. Ibid., p. 236.

3. Ibid.

4. Katherine Doob Sakenfeld, "Numbers," as found in *Women's Bible Commentary, Expanded Edition, with Apocrypha*, edited by Carol A. Newsom and Sharon H. Ringe, editors (Louisville: Westminster John Knox Press, 1998), pp. 54-55.

# six

# Mary, the mother of Jesus

# We Are Meant to Become a Word of Wisdom

*As people gather for this celebration of Evening Prayer,[1] they are welcomed by soft candlelight in the entrance area and throughout the worship space. Musicians playing reflective music set a welcoming tone as well, and greeters offer them programs. Central to the worship space is the large Christ Candle and a large Book of Scripture, adorned in the colors of the season. (This might be on a stand, next to the candle.)*

*Ministers:* Mary, leader, reader, cantor, and musicians

*Materials:* large candle, large book of the scriptures

## Introductory Rites

CALL TO WORSHIP                                          *Please stand*

Leader:     "In the beginning was the Word, +

All:          and the Word was with God."[2]

Leader:     "Now the Word of God came to me saying,
              before I formed you in the womb I knew you,
              and before you were born I consecrated you;
              I appointed you a prophet to the nations."[3]

All: "Then Mary said,
'Here am I, the servant of the Lord;
let it be with me according to your word.'"[4]

Leader: "And the Word became flesh

All: and lived among us."[5]

OPENING HYMN
• • • • • • • • • • • • •

"God of Day and God of Darkness," text by Marty Haugen, tune is "The Sacred Harp," GIA Publications, Inc., © 1985.

or

"Here I Am, Lord," text and tune by Dan Schutte, Daniel L. Schutte and New Dawn Music, © 1981.

or

"Night of Silence," text and tune by Daniel Kantor, GIA Publications, Inc., © 1984. (This is especially appropriate for the Advent/Christmas/Epiphany season.)

# Liturgy of the Word
• • • • • • • • • • • • • • • • • • • • • • • • • • • • • • • • • • • • • • • • • •

ISAIAH 42:1-4                                              *Please be seated*
• • • • • • • • • • • •

*(Substitute "she" for "he," since Mary serves as our guide)*

Here is my servant, whom I uphold,
my chosen, in whom my soul delights;
I have put my spirit upon her;
she will bring forth justice to the nations.
She will not cry or lift up her voice,
or make it heard in the street;
a bruised reed she will not break,
and a dimly burning wick she will not quench;
she will faithfully bring forth justice.
She will not grow faint or be crushed
until she has established justice in the earth;
and the coastlands wait for her teaching.

PSALM 116

. . . . . . . . .

"The Name of God," text and tune by David Haas, GIA Publications, Inc., © 1987.

LUKE 1:26-38

. . . . . . . . . . .

CONSCIOUSNESS EXAMEN

*(led by Mary, based upon her life experiences)*

. . . . . . . . . . . . . . . . . . . . . . . . . . . . . .

*Mary invites everyone into the silence, to listen prayerfully, and to reflect on the questions she raises.*

## The Call

. . . . . . . . . . . . . . . . . . . . . . . . . . . . . . . . . . . . . . . . . . . . . . . . . . . . .

It all began in prayer. In a moment of intimacy. Of knowing and being known. Of trusting—like a babe in arms, safe and secure—and being trusted. Of being set free, like soaring on the wings of an eagle . . . or on the mighty arm of our God, who brought us out of slavery in Egypt, to be God's very own . . . a "treasured possession" and "a holy nation."[6] Yes, it all began in prayer. And in that moment of gentle earthquake, my life would be forever changed. By the assurance that I had "found favor with God." With the question of giving birth to "a son," whom I would name Jesus.

"How can this be?" was all I could say in the moment. But other questions began to "trouble the water" of giving birth. What would this ask of me? For I knew about the demands of God on the ones who had found favor with God—all men, I might add. Noah.[7] Moses.[8] Gideon.[9] Samuel.[10] In the cases of Moses and Gideon, it was for the deliverance of Israel, no less! Was I up to it? How would this change my life? And, besides all that, who could possibly understand? My parents? Joseph? They were kind and just, but could they understand this?[11] Was there anyone else? Ah, I had it! My relative Elizabeth! Though years and miles apart . . . she from the hill country of Judea, the rugged spine where prophecy was never totally forgotten . . . and I up north here in Galilee . . . we were intimates. Soul sisters. I decided to do the unthinkable, to make that nearly hundred mile trek alone to be with my Elizabeth. A just woman. A wise woman. A woman whose compassion was forged out of the fiery furnace of yearning for a son . . . enduring the shame of barrenness . . . and finally bearing the son she thought she would never have. Elizabeth would understand.

Yes, God, "let it be with me according to your word."

*Pause*

What are the demands that have come out of your prayer life? What motivates you to say "Yes" to God? Who would understand?

*Silence*

PSALM 116 (*sung refrain*)
· · · · · · · · · · · · · · · · · ·

"I will take the cup of life, I will call God's name, all my days."

## The Birth
· · · · · · · · · · · · · · · · · · · · · · · · · · · · · · · · · · · · · · · · · · ·

I *must* tell you about the birth of Jesus. Already people are putting me on some kind of pedestal, as though his birth was different, somehow. As though his birth was not the same miracle as every human birth. For every birth is seeded by God. And every birth takes time . . . planning . . . forming . . . shaping . . . and growing.

Oh, how that growing time with Elizabeth helped! We laughed and cried. We poured out our hearts, our hopes, and our fears. We remembered the God of our prophets. The God of fiery, yet compassionate, Elijah. The God of plucky, persistent Hannah . . . of Jeremiah . . . and of Isaiah of the exile, who set my heart to song. The God whose ways turn things upside down, who "brings low" and also "exalts," who "lifts the needy from the ash heap."[12] Who "destroys and overthrows" arrogance, but "builds up" faithfulness.[13] Who cries "out like a woman in labor" and leads "the blind by a road they do not know," "who makes a way in the sea, a path in the mighty waters," always doing "a new thing" for the faithful ones of Israel.[14] And we vowed that our sons would know this God, as well.

When my time came, I gave birth, in the way of every woman. In water breaking open, and body and blood poured out. In mess and confusion, noise and chaos, fear and courage. In uncertainty and pondering. How was it, that right from the beginning, there was no place to lay his head, except in a manger, a feeding trough for animals? How was it that shepherds, the outcast of our society, were first to worship Jesus? And, on the special occasion of his circumcision, what did Simeon—that oracle of God—know about Jesus that I had yet to learn? What did he mean that Jesus was God's "salvation," "a light for revelation to the Gentiles"?[15] What did he mean, when he looked deep into my eyes, with those troubling words, "and a sword will pierce your own soul, too"?[16] This birth was only the beginning; that was all I knew.

*Pause*

What has been your experience of giving birth, to a person or a creative endeavor of any kind? And who has God become for you, in the process?

*Silence*

PSALM 116 *(sung refrain)*
. . . . . . . . . . . . . . . . . .

"I will take the cup of life, I will call God's name, all my days."

## The "Stretch Marks" of Birthing
. . . . . . . . . . . . . . . . . . . . . . . . . . . . . . . . . . . . . . . . . . . . . . . . . .

Giving birth leaves its mark. We are never the same again. And, we learn soon enough that this precious new life does not belong to us. Jesus was very clear about this. He had a mission, well beyond his immediate family: "to bring good news to the poor," to "proclaim release to the captives and recovery of sight to the blind, to let the oppressed go free, to proclaim the year of the Lord's favor.[17] Despite resistance, and even rage, right from the beginning. It led, of course, to the cross.

How can I ever forget that terrible Friday? I was so thirsty, so very thirsty . . . from the heat and the brutality, the noise of the crowd and the pounding in my head. And then I heard him say, "I thirst," and my heart broke. He had always been thirsty, as far back as I can remember. For life! For people to care about each other . . . and to *know* the God of love! (*Pause*) How could I ever make sense of all this horror? How would I ever forgive his friends who deserted him? The disciples who never seemed to understand, who continued to argue among themselves about who was greatest? What could I ever say to Peter, who denied him . . . three times?

But, then, as we waited together in that upper room—fearful and faithful, frail and powerful, visionary and practical, righteous and self-righteous, doubting and risking, suffering and loving—I began to be stretched one more time. Yes, I saw, one more time, how ferocious, but fragile, was Peter's love for Jesus. And I listened, one more time, to the whisper that had, by now, made a home in me. And said "Yes" one more time, to becoming a word of forgiveness . . . a word of challenge . . . a word of comfort . . . a word of hope . . . a word of life . . . a word of wisdom.

*Pause*

What does it mean to you to follow Jesus?

*Silence*

## GOSPEL CANTICLE

"Holy Is Your Name," text by David Haas (based on Luke 1:46-55, the Magnificat), tune is Irish traditional Wild Mountain Thyme, arranged by David Haas, GIA Publications, Inc., © 1989.

# Ritual of Serving God's Word

## INTRODUCTION

Leader:     Isaiah, prophetic servant of God, spoke for God in this way: My word "shall not return to me empty, but it shall accomplish that which I purpose, and succeed in the thing for which I sent it."[18] Mary, prophetic servant of God, put human flesh on those words in a most unique way. She not only birthed God's Word but she birthed her own unique word as well. It is our life's task to become a word of God, in good times and in bad. To listen attentively to God's call, as Mary did, in all the intimate moments of prayer. To be consummated with God's dreams, as Mary was, that they might grow and live within us, until we are ready to give them birth. To bear the stretch marks of birthing, as Mary did, by becoming the person that God had in mind from the very beginning. If you are ready to become God's servant by bearing God's prophetic word, please respond as follows.

## COMMITMENT TO SERVE GOD BY SPEAKING OUR UNIQUE WORD

Leader: What is your name?

All: My name is _____. *Each "word" is pronounced at the same time.*

Leader: Are you willing to serve God by being true to your own word, listening for it in silence, and continuing to pronounce it, even in the hard times?

All: I am.

## INVITATION TO REVERENCE THE BOOK AS A SIGN OF COMMITMENT

Leader: As a sign of commitment to our promises, I will begin the process of reverently touching and then passing on the Living Word of God, as found in this book. Please take all the time you need. The last person may return the Living Word to its place of honor in our midst.

## MUSIC DURING THE RITUAL

"Gospel Acclamation" for the *Mass of Creation*, with all verses, text, and music from the *Mass of Creation* by Marty Haugen, GIA Publications, Inc., © 1984.

## PRAYERS FOR THE WORLD

Leader: For whom shall we pray, that others might speak their "word"? Please respond by saying, "Servant God, hear our prayer."

## "THE LORD'S PRAYER" *(A word that Jesus gave us, Aramaic version)*[19]

O Birther! Father-Mother of the Cosmos,
focus your light within us—make it useful.
Create your reign of unity now.
Your one desire then acts with ours,
as in all light, so in all forms.
Grant what we need each day in bread and insight.

Loose the cords of mistakes binding us,
as we release the strands we hold of others' guilt.
Don't let surface things delude us,
but free us from what holds us back.
From you is born all ruling will, the power and life to do,
the song that beautifies all, from age to age it renews.
Truly—power to these statements—
may they be the ground from which all my actions grow. Amen.

## THE SIGN OF PEACE

# Closing Rites

### BLESSING                                              *Please stand*

*The assembly forms a "left" and a "right," facing each other. Then with hands outstretched in blessing, each prays a blessing on the other, so that they give and receive the same words at the same time.*

Go forth to become your own special word.
Listen, deeply and intently, as God speaks,
"Be still, and know that I am God."[20]

Go forth, in trust.
"Blessed are they who believe that there will be
a fulfillment of what was spoken to them by God."[21]

Go forth in the words of Jesus, the Christ,
God's ultimate Word in our midst,
"Blessed are those who hear the word of God and obey it!"[22]

Go forth in the power of God's Word.
Listen for it! Pronounce it! Become it!
Amen! Alleluia! Yes, let it be!

## CLOSING HYMN

● ● ● ● ● ● ● ● ● ● ● ●

"Jubilate Deo" (Rejoice in God, all the earth. Serve the Lord with gladness), in a round (text based on Psalm 100), Taize community, 1978; tune by Jacques Berthier, GIA Publications, Inc., © 1979.

## NOTES

● ● ● ● ●

1.  You will note this is a modified version of Evening Prayer. Normally the Liturgy of the Word for Evening Prayer includes at least two psalms and a short reading. However, the two readings I have selected are essential to the reflection; therefore, I have reordered the rite with a psalm in between the readings.

2.  John 1:1a, b.

3.  Jeremiah 1:4-5.

4.  Luke 1:38.

5.  John 1:14a.

6.  See Exodus 19:3-6, the words of God to Moses.

7.  See Genesis 6:8. This information—and the names of others who found favor with God—is taken from Barbara E. Reid, *Choosing the Better Part?: Women in the Gospel of Luke* (Collegeville, MN: The Liturgical Press, a Michael Glazier Book, 1996), p. 67; hereafter referred to as Reid.

8.  See Exodus 33:12-17.

9.  See Judges 6:17.

10. See 1 Samuel 2:26.

11. As a good Jew, Joseph would know he could have her stoned. See Deuteronomy 22:23-24.

12. See 1 Samuel 2:7-8.

13. See Jeremiah 1:10.

14. See Isaiah 42:14, 16; 43:16, 19.

15. See Luke 2:29-32.

16. See Luke 2:34-35.

17. See Luke 4:18-19.

18. Isaiah 55:11.

19. Taken from Neil Douglas-Klotz, *Prayers of the Cosmos: Meditations on the Aramaic Words of Jesus* (New York: Harper & Row, 1990).

20. See Psalm 46:10a.

21. Based upon Elizabeth's blessing of Mary, Luke 1:45.

22. Luke 11:28.

# Mary, A Word of Wisdom

The Word of God is alive! Inviting. Urging. Forming and shaping. Challenging. Comforting. Transforming. It is a Word of Wisdom. Those who hear God's Word and act upon it are family with Jesus . . . serving God and God's children.

If anyone knew that, it was Mary, the mother of Jesus. Mary, a complex woman of contradictions, in scripture and tradition. Imaged in so many hearts, in so many different ways. A woman given a multiplicity of titles, but known from the beginning as "God bearer." During the Middle Ages she became the gentle mother one could count on, a mother tinged with the divine (Isaiah 49:15), mediator for fallen humanity to a God perceived as distant, even stern. Some have placed her on a pedestal beyond human reach. And many have praised her prayerful pondering.

Yet, Christian feminists today question why Mary has been known more for her silent reflection than for her passionate proclamation of radical justice in the Magnificat (Luke 1:46-55). Why does her passivity often come to mind rather than her strength in becoming an unwed mother and a refugee in exile as a teenager? Why has she remained so invisible at Pentecost, even though Luke names her alone among the women who are present indeed (Acts 1:12-14)?[1] Why has the tradition connected her service with being sexually "pure"?

This is not the place to answer all these questions about Mary, but simply to raise them. This is not the place to document all the twists and turns of Marian tradition, for that has already been capably done.[2] Rather, this is the place to explore Mary, "servant of the Lord," as a Word of Wisdom, a model for us in putting flesh on God's Word. This will be done by placing Mary in her context as a faithful Jewish woman, by describing her development in scripture, and by allowing her to speak to us today through the lens of the Second Vatican Council, so that we, too, might wrestle with becoming a Word of Wisdom.

## MARY IN CONTEXT: A FAITHFUL, PIOUS JEW

Whether or not she could read, Mary knew the Law and the Prophets. For she was a faithful Jew. There is no way we can be certain of her favorite passages, but it's plausible to imagine this. As a woman of the lower classes, a Jew under Roman control, she might well have been deeply moved by the majestic, poignant poetry of Second Isaiah.[3] This was the prophet who offered hope—where none existed—to Jewish exiles in Babylon. This was the prophet who proclaimed that the God of creation, who "stretches out the heavens like a curtain," is the God of salvation.[4] This is the prophet who assured the people of a glorious homecoming in lofty Exodus imagery, like a new creation. "See, the Lord God comes with might, and his arm rules for him; . . . He will feed his flock like a shepherd; he will gather the lambs in his arms, and carry them in his bosom. . . ."[5] This is the prophet who is not afraid to look suffering in the eye, plumbing the depths of the exile experience through his "Suffering Servant Songs."[6] From the gentle servant of the first poem—a teacher who faithfully, persistently, quietly brings forth justice—the servant gradually is immersed in rejection and abandonment. In the end, the servant's ministry is one of atonement, taking on the sins of all. And, in the process, the servant becomes a "light to the nations," radiating God's goodness, gathering people together in praise of God's Name.

Scholars have long wrestled with the identity of this "Suffering Servant." Is it the faithful remnant of Israel? Or, a Jeremiah-type individual who plumbs the depths of suffering? For Christians, later on, this is none other than Jesus. And yet, for those who are family to Jesus, does not the family share in the ministry of the "Suffering Servant"? And would not Mary, as pre-eminent among the family, reveal the servant's light, especially as the gentle, prophetic teacher of justice in the first Song? Consider these questions as we briefly explore what scripture says of Mary.

## WHAT DOES SCRIPTURE SAY?

The canonical gospels move from a largely negative picture of Mary in Mark to positive, though different, portraits by Matthew, Luke, and John. In Mark there is no infancy narrative. His account mentions Mary in only two stories: the true family of Jesus (3:31-35) and the rejection of Jesus by the folks in his hometown of Nazareth (6:1-6a). Although Matthew and Luke offer parallel accounts, they both soften Mark's view. For Mark is critical of Jesus' biological family—mother, sisters, and brothers. According to Mark, they are so disturbed by the crowds around Jesus that they cannot even eat (3:20). And, painfully aware of the whispers about Jesus, that he "has gone out of his mind" (3:21), they stand *outside* the crowd, calling to him, trying to restrain him. In response, Jesus is blunt. *They* are the ones who are outside the family. For the family of Jesus is no longer simply biological; his family is engaged in doing "the will of God" (3:35). In the hometown rejection story, the slur of Jesus' presumed illegitimacy adds to the negativity. "Is not this the carpenter, the son of Mary?" (6:3).

Matthew's most significant contributions regarding Mary are to be found in his infancy narrative (chapters one and two), the gospel in miniature.[7] There is no mistake: Mary is definitely part of Jesus' family. For he begins the entire gospel with a genealogy of Jesus; and he takes the highly unusual step of including five women in the ancestry, the last of whom is "Mary, of whom Jesus was born, who is called the Messiah" (1:16). Each of these women—Tamar, Rahab, Ruth, "the wife of Uriah" (Bathsheba, not named in the genealogy), and Mary—gives birth in a most unusual way.[8] Some are suspect and some are outsiders, but all faithfully participate in the divine plan, becoming family with Jesus. Finally, in the infancy narrative, Mary is caught up, along with Joseph and Jesus, in the tempest of power struggles that will culminate in the Passion. It is only in Matthew's account that the family becomes refugees, fleeing to Egypt until it is safe to return. She knows firsthand, as a teenager, the suffering of exiles from Isaiah's time down to the present day.

Luke's portrait of Mary is drawn in loving detail. She is a model disciple: one who hears the word of God, reflects on it, and says "Yes" . . . again and again and again. Indeed, she is crucial to Luke's Gospel overture or infancy narrative, his first two chapters.[9] When we encounter her for the first time, in the annunciation story, she is named as "favored one," which gives her pause. For she knows that God demanded great things from favored ones, all men, before her—Noah, Moses, Gideon, and Samuel.[10] But she says "Yes" and names herself "servant of the Lord" (1:38).

The word in Greek is a hard one, *doulos*, which means slave. Where is the merit in such a word? Especially for African Americans . . . and all who have been shunted to one side, like women in general? But scripture places her in good company . . . with Jesus . . . with Isaiah's Suffering Servant . . . and with Abraham, Isaac, Jacob, Moses, Joshua, Hannah (mother of Samuel), and David before them. And, Luke reveals her as a *prophetic* servant as she proclaims God's liberating reversals in the "Magnificat" (1:46-55). Could it be that the essence of Jesus' vision of his mission, a proclamation of jubilee justice, was learned at the gentle knee of his mother, his first teacher?[11] Finally, Luke suggests—through the words of the prophet Simeon—that she will become a suffering servant, not unlike Jesus, "and a sword will pierce your own soul too" (Luke 2:35).

In John's Gospel, there is no infancy narrative, for "in the beginning was the Word. . . . And the Word became flesh and lived among us" (John 1:1, 14). But Mary is significant in two places, at the wedding feast of Cana and at the foot of the Cross. What kind of a woman do we find at the wedding? She is compassionate, for the young couple has run out of wine. She is understanding, not only of their predicament but of Jesus' authority. She is empowering, intending to draw out all that Jesus has to offer. She is confident in her judgment and in the son she knows so well. It is true that Jesus refuses to be pushed beyond his own understanding of his mission. But he then takes charge, believing that his betrothal to Israel is about to be made public. He *knows* that he is the true bridegroom of abundant life. But there were those who did not accept him. . . . So, at the foot of the Cross, stood a woman in profound pain. At the foot of the Cross, stood a woman with the strength and stamina, courage and compassion, faithfulness and integrity to form genuine Christian community. As Jesus poured out his life, he poured out his Spirit on this woman and the beloved disciple. As the blood and water flowed from his side, the water of birth broke open upon the first Christian community, one based on love and mutuality of service, for the purpose of bearing fruit that will last, abundant life.[12]

## MARY, FROM THE PERSPECTIVE OF THE SECOND VATICAN COUNCIL

And she is still there, in every birthing of the church. In their Spirit-filled wisdom, members of the Second Vatican Council chose to include Mary in the document on church, *Lumen Gentium (A Light to the Nations)*, rather than to write a complete and separate doctrine on Mary. Yes, at this Council, there was a sound from heaven like a strong driving wind that shook the preconceptions of being church. Church was now named a Mystery, "in the nature of a sacrament—a sign and instrument, that is of communion with God and of unity among all" people.[13] On its pilgrim path, this sacrament of church was to look to Mary as its model. For, "as St. Ambrose taught, the Mother of God is a type of the church in the order of faith, charity, and perfect union with Christ."[14] She is "pre-eminent" and "a wholly unique member of the church," an "outstanding model in faith and charity."[15] The church is to hear the voice of God, listen deeply and reflect on it, bear and give birth to God's Word, just as Mary did. In this way, it becomes a sacrament, revealing the light of Jesus to the nations, just as Jesus revealed the nature of God.

In the wake of Vatican II, theologians like Gustavo Gutierrez in Latin America put on a new pair of glasses. They grappled with the theology of *Lumen Gentium* through the eyes of those who are poor. For Gutierrez, to say that the church is sacrament, revealing the face of God, is to say that the church exists "for others."[16] And those others are "the poor," the new subjects of God's action, the people in whom God is to be encountered. The church's call, therefore, is to denounce sin in the form of oppressive structures, poverty, and all that keeps people down; it is, at the same time, a call to announce God's liberating love by identifying with those in poverty so as to transform the structures of sin. This can only be done by critically reflecting upon and living the gospel in solidarity with the poor.[17] Such a process has unleashed a surging stream, several forms of liberation theology, water breaking open the stories of those on the underside, lifting up the voices of all who have not been heard, so that *all* might have life.[18]

Mary knew all about this. When she said "Yes" to bearing God's Son, she did not know if her betrothed would discard her. She gave birth in a stable. She lived in exile. She watched the execution of her innocent son. But she knew the God of liberating reversals. And she served that God as courageous prophet—taking in, pondering, and acting upon God's Word—in solidarity with those who suffer. In the end, she not only taught and companioned *the* Suffering Servant, but she became one herself. And, in the process, she became a Word of Wisdom for every age.

Now it is up to us, the church today, disciples of Jesus, the "Suffering Servant." With every annunciation, we are called by name to give birth to God's Word in some form. We are "favored," given some responsibility for the world in which we live. What is the name by which God calls each of us? With whom are we to stand in solidarity? What will it cost? In short, how is God inviting us to become a Word of Wisdom for our day?

## SOME RESOURCES
. . . . . . . . . . . . . . . .

Brown, Raymond E., S.S. *The Gospel According to John: The Anchor Bible*. Garden City, NY: Doubleday & Company, Inc., 1966.

Chopp, Rebecca S. *The Praxis of Suffering: An Interpretation of Liberation and Political Theologies*. Maryknoll, NY: Orbis Books, 1986.

Cunneen, Sally. *In Search of Mary: The Woman and the Symbol*. New York: Ballantine Books, 1996.

Flannery, Austin, O.P., General Editor. *Vatican Council II. The Conciliar and Post Conciliar Documents*. "Dogmatic Constitution on the Church/ Lumen Gentium," Chapter VIII, "Our Lady," pp. 413-423. Northport, NY: Costello Publishing Company, Inc., 1975 and 1984.

Gaventa, Beverly Roberts. *Mary: Glimpses of the Mother of Jesus*. Columbia, SC: University of South Carolina, 1999.

Johnson, Ann. *Miryam of Jerusalem, Teacher of the Disciples*. Notre Dame: Ave Maria Press, 1991.

McKenna, Megan. *Not Counting Women and Children*. Maryknoll, NY: Orbis Books, 1994, pp. 91-118.

Newsom, Carol A. and Sharon H. Ringe, editors. *Women's Bible Commentary, Expanded Edition, with Apocrypha*. Louisville, KY: Westminster John Knox Press, 1998.

Polan, Gregory J., O.S.B. "Portraits of Second Isaiah's Servant." In *The Bible Today*, March/April 2001, Vol. 39, #2. Collegeville, MN: The Liturgical Press, 2001.

Reid, Barbara E. *Choosing the Better Part?: Women in the Gospel of Luke*. Collegeville, MN: Liturgical Press, 1996.

Schneiders, Sandra M. *Written That You May Believe: Encountering Jesus in the Fourth Gospel*. New York: The Crossroad Publishing Company, a Herder & Herder Book, 1999.

## NOTES
. . . . .

1. Feminist scholars today are calling into question the traditional belief that Luke was favorable toward women. While he does include a number of women in Luke/Acts, they become increasingly silent, women without a voice. Some scholars suggest that he is presenting women in a way that will not "rock the boat" of Roman society. See, for example, Barbara E. Reid, *Choosing the Better Part?: Women in the Gospel of Luke* (Collegeville, MN: Liturgical Press, 1996).

2. See, for example, Sally Cunneen, *In Search of Mary: the Woman and the Symbol* (New York: Ballantine Books, 1996).

3. Second Isaiah is credited with chapters 40-55 of that book, offering hope to Jewish exiles in Babylon in the sixth century before Jesus.

4. Isaiah 40:22.

5. Isaiah 40:10a, 11a, b.

6. The "Suffering Servant Songs" include Isaiah 42:1-4 (some include through verse 7 or 9), 49:1-6 (some include through verse 7, 9, or 13), 50:4-9 (some include verses 10 and 11), and 52:13–53:12.

7. These two chapters highlight the person of Jesus. For Jesus is identified as Messiah (1:1, 16, 18), the son of David (1:10), and Emmanuel or "God is with us" (1:23). It is here that the universality of Jesus is first presented. It is here that the storm clouds first gather around Jesus, foreshadowing his passion. For King Herod and "all Jerusalem" are disturbed and frightened as the magi inquire about Jesus (2:3). Herod fears the loss of power, but his plot to elicit information about the child from the magi is thwarted; they are waned in a dream not to return to Herod and instead to go home by another road (2:12). But Herod is so obsessed with power that he orders the massacre of the innocents in and around Bethlehem, and Rachel is heard weeping for her children "because they are no more" (2:18). Finally, the magi offer prophetic gifts, beyond their knowing; myrrh is a resin used for anointing and embalming (for Jesus, the crucified king).

8. Megan McKenna gives a powerful account of these women in her book *Not Counting Women and Children* (Maryknoll, NY: Orbis Books, 1994), pp. 91-118.

9. This is also a gospel in miniature, for Luke presents his main themes, such as: 1) the return of prophesy and the coming of the Holy Spirit with the birth of Jesus, 2) Jesus as Christ, Savior ("Saving Instrument"), Son of God and fulfillment of God's promises, 3) God's preference for the lowly and the hungry and God's upside-down ways of relating with humanity (Mary's Magnificat and the proclamation of the Good News to the shepherds), 4) the universality of God's saving action in Jesus, 5) Jesus as food for the world (Jesus is laid in a manger, an animal trough).

10. See Barbara E. Reid, *Choosing the Better Part?: Women in the Gospel of Luke* (Collegeville, MN: The Liturgical Press, a Michael Glazier Book, 1996), p. 67.

11. See Luke 4:16-21.

12. See Sandra M. Schneiders, *Written That You May Believe: Encountering Jesus in the Fourth Gospel* (New York: The Crossroad Publishing Company, A Herder & Herder Book, 1999). See especially pp. 162-179, where she explores John's community as a community of friends, where inequality has been erased.

13. Austin Flannery, O.P., General Editor, *Vatican Council II. The Conciliar and Post Conciliar Documents. "Dogmatic Constitution on the Church/ Lumen*

*Gentium"* (Northport, NY: Costello Publishing Company, Inc., 1975 and 1984), #1, p. 350; hereafter referred to as *LG.*

14. *LG* #63, p. 419.

15. *LG* #53, p. 414.

16. Gustavo Gutierrez, *A Theology of Liberation,* ed. and trans. Sister Caridad Inda and John Eagleson (Maryknoll, NY: Orbis Books, 1973), p. 260, as found in Rebecca S. Chopp, *The Praxis of Suffering* (Maryknoll, NY: Orbis Books, 1986), p. 55; hereafter referred to as Chopp.

17. Chopp, pp. 56-57.

18. One of these streams of liberation theology is feminist scripture scholarship today.

# seven

# A WOMAN WHO ANOINTED JESUS

# We Give Courageously of Our Very Selves

*As people enter the worship space, all their senses are touched. The worship space is "beautiful," with some fragrant flowers at various locations throughout the worship space. Candles are in evidence, as well, if it is evening. The musicians are playing some tender, inviting music. The main focus is a table, covered with a lovely cloth, on which is a glass bowl of perfumed oil. The perfume is symbolic of the Spirit of God, wafting everywhere, unable to be contained or controlled. There is also a large lighted candle on the table. If someone has an appropriate flask, that is placed on the table, as well, next to the perfumed oil.*

Ministers:   *leader, storyteller, reader, cantor, and musicians*

Materials:   *table covered with a tablecloth, large bowl of perfumed oil, flowers, candles*

## Introductory Rites

CALL TO WORSHIP                                    *Please stand*

Leader:   Where chaos threatens and storm clouds descend,

All:      let there be the light of lavish love.

Leader:   Where shame surges upon the shore of life,

---

111

| | |
|---|---|
| All: | let there be the shattering power of a gentle touch. |
| Leader: | Where pain and death arrive with exclamation points, |
| All: | let there be the irrepressible force of new life. |
| Leader: | Where ugliness and folly threaten to reign, |
| All: | let there be beauty and wisdom, enough to prevail. |
| Leader: | Where beginnings fail, |
| All: | let there be beginning again. |

## OPENING HYMN
• • • • • • • • • • •

"Shake Up the Morning," text by John Bell, tune "Shake Up" by John Bell, Iona Community, GIA Publications, Inc., © 1987.

## Liturgy of the Word
• • • • • • • • • • • • • • • • • • • • • • • • • • • • • • • • • • • • • • • • • • •

MARK 14:1-9[1] *(Reader proclaims)*                    *Please be seated*
• • • • • • • • • • • • • • • • • • • • • •

It was now two days before the Passover and the feast of Unleavened Bread. And the chief priests and the scribes were seeking how to arrest him by stealth, and kill him, for they said, "Not during the feast, lest there be a tumult of the people."

And while he was at Bethany in the house of Simon the leper, as he sat at table, a woman came with an alabaster flask of ointment of pure nard, very costly, and she broke the flask and poured it over his head. But there were some who said to themselves indignantly, "Why was the ointment thus wasted? For this ointment might have been sold for more than three hundred denarii, and given to the poor." And they reproached her. But Jesus said, "Let her alone; why do you trouble her? She has done a beautiful thing to me. For you always have the poor with you, and whenever you will, you can do good to them but you will not always have me. She has done what she could; she has anointed my body beforehand for burying. And truly, I say to you, wherever the gospel is preached in the whole world, what she has done will be told in memory of her."

## REFLECTION *(Leader or a Storyteller, or in three voices)*

*Voice One:*

Jesus knew. And so did "a woman."
It was a beautiful thing to see,
the intensity of his pain . . . alone
matched by the extravagance of her love.

The storm clouds had gathered . . .
searing tension, certain foreboding,
a plot nearly hatched among religious leaders
who found him "too much," a gut-wrenching offense.
Surely, slowly, the shroud was descending.

Until . . . "a woman" broke into the dinner party,
uninvited, unnamed, unwanted by nearly everybody,
except one, an outsider, the man on whom she poured herself out.
Did she consider that another outsider, the host,
Simon, the leper, might understand? No matter.

*Voice Two:*

Who *is* this woman?
A disciple, perhaps?
Nobody was surprised by her presence, it seemed,
only shaken up by her action.
Of this alone are we certain . . . she had resources, financial and
  otherwise.

*Voice Three:*

It is a beautiful thing to see
Woman-Vision,
Spirit set free to know and to understand,
heart-sight etched by many a sting of rejection,
released now for ministry to Suffering Servant Messiah.

It is a beautiful thing to see
Woman-Strength,
Woman standing tall, over and behind
the One she was about to anoint, by choice
deliberately, passionately pouring out all her resources.

It is a beautiful thing to see
Woman-Truth, in a long line of prophets,
otherwise male, like Samuel of old.
Who "took a vial of oil," poured it on the head of Saul,
and proclaimed him "ruler over his people Israel."[2]

*Voice Two:*

It is a beautiful thing to see
Woman-Wisdom,
confident, courageous, assured and assertive.
Who intuitively knows, it is by her that "kings reign,
and rulers decree what is just."[3]

It is a beautiful thing to see
Woman-Disciple, in the ideal, according to Mark.
She sees, hears, and understands, the "Son of Man came
not to be served but to serve, and to give his life a ransom for many."[4]
Unlike all those who continue to argue, "Who is greatest among us?"

It is a beautiful thing to see
Woman-Witness. Jesus saw . . . and appreciated.
For he recognized a soul mate, and proclaimed about her,
"wherever the gospel is preached in the whole world,
what she has done will be told in memory of her."

*Voice One:*

It is a beautiful thing to see
Woman-Priest.
Her healing hands penetrate depths,
to the core of his lonely exile;
her very being imparts God's irrepressible embrace.

It is a beautiful thing to see
Woman-Sacrament.
Passion, compassion, life poured out,
"bridled only by love."[5]
"Do this in remembrance of me."[6]

*Silence*

"I Will Give What I Have," words and music The Iona Community, GIA Publications, Inc., © 1988. *This is based upon the same story, as told in Matthew 26:3-13.*

## Ritual of Anointing the Body of Christ
• • • • • • • • • • • • • • • • • • • • • • • • • • • • • • • • • • • • • • • • •

### INTRODUCTION *(Leader)*
• • • • • • • • • • • • • • • • • • • • •

The person of Jesus was hurting. And the Body of Christ is still in pain. From acts of terrorism, and violence lurking everywhere, even within. From struggles to make ends meet and to "be there" for children. From bullying in schools and addiction to drugs. From being ignored . . . or abused. From all the imprints of life's wounds. Yes, the Body of Christ is hurting and in need of lavish love.

It took a woman of courage to do as Jesus would have done . . . to pour herself out for another, regardless of the cost. Before we, ourselves, are anointed for this kind of courage, we remember this woman-anointer, who loved as Jesus loves.

## Litany of Remembrance
• • • • • • • • • • • • • • • • • • • • • • • • • • • • • • • • • • • • • • • • •

| | |
|---|---|
| Leader: | Without price, |
| All: | without regard for status, |
| Leader: | without regard for belonging, |
| All: | without regard for wealth, |
| Leader: | with understanding and compassion, |
| All: | with prodigal abundance, |
| Leader: | with beauty, strength, and courage, |
| All: | risking everything for another, |
| Leader: | breaking taboos for the sake of healing, |
| All: | trusting in God, |

Leader:     to serve one in need,

All:        "Do this in memory of me."

## BLESSING OF THE PERFUMED OIL
. . . . . . . . . . . . . . . . . . . . . . . . . . .

*Leader invites everyone to extend an arm in blessing, while praying together:*

Lavish, loving God,
outpoured for the life of the world,
we ask that our memories be fortified
so that this fragrant oil may become for us
a sacrament of healing and vision, compassion and strength,
truth and beauty, wisdom and the fullness of discipleship.
We pray all this in the name of Jesus, who is beauty outpoured. Amen.

## ANOINTING: THAT WE MIGHT GIVE OUR ALL
. . . . . . . . . . . . . . . . . . . . . . . . . . . . . . . .

Leader:     And now, as you are ready, please come forward to be
            anointed for mission. The Leader and Reader will anoint
            one another and then anoint you on the eyes, the forehead,
            and hands, with these words: "May God give you eyes to
            see the wounded Christ *(anointing of the eyes)*, the will and
            heart to remember the broken Body of Christ *(anointing of
            the forehead)*, by doing a beautiful thing *(anointing of the
            hands)*."

## MUSIC DURING THE ANOINTING RITUAL
. . . . . . . . . . . . . . . . . . . . . . . . . . . . . .

"Ubi Caritas," text 1 Corinthians 13:2-8, Taize Community, 1978, tune
by Jacques Berthier, Les Presses de Taize, GIA Publications, Inc., ©
1979.

or

"Take, O Take Me As I Am," from the Iona Collection *Come All You
People*, Wild Goose Resource Group, Iona Community, Glasgow,
Scotland, GIA Publications, Inc., © 1995.

or

"All I Ask of You," text and music by Gregory Norbet, O.S.B., The
Benedictine Foundation of the State of Vermont, Inc., © 1973.

# Closing Rites

· · · · · · · · · · · · · · · · · · · · · · · · · · · · · · · · · · · · · · · · · · ·

## BLESSING                                                    *Please stand*

· · · · · · · ·

*The assembly faces one another, with "left" facing "right," lifting an arm in blessing as these words are said to one another:*

Go in beauty,
Beauty before you, beauty behind you,
Beauty above you, beauty below you,
Beauty within and around you.

Go in Christ,
Christ before you, Christ behind you,
Christ above you, Christ below you,
Christ within and around you.

Do this in memory of her.
Do this in memory of me.

## CLOSING HYMN

· · · · · · · · · · · ·

"God Has Chosen Me," Bernadette Farrell, OCP Publications, © 1990.

## NOTES

· · · · ·

1. I am using the translation from the Nestle-Aland Greek English New Testament. It accurately translates the Greek, "She has done a beautiful thing to me," rather than the NRSV translation, "She has performed a good service for me."

2. See 1 Samuel 9:27–10:1.

3. See Proverbs 8:15.

4. See Mark 10:45.

5. I owe this beautiful phrase to J. Philip Newell, as found on p. 14 of his book, *Celtic Benediction: Morning and Night Prayer* (Grand Rapids, MI: William B. Eerdmans Publishing Co., 2000).

6. In the Gospels of Mark and Matthew, Jesus leaves this phrase out of his "words of institution" at the Last Supper (see Mark 14:22-25/Matthew 26:26-29). He has already spoken them, with regard to this woman's actions.

# The Woman in Mark's Gospel Who Anointed Jesus on the Head

## (Mark 14:3-9)

She is a mystery. She is an unknown woman, appearing ever so briefly in Mark's Gospel. Her only other gospel appearance comes later, in Matthew.[1] In both instances she creates a stir, barging into a dinner party at the home of Simon the leper. In both instances, she dares to stand behind and above Jesus, anointing him on the head. In both instances, the fierce storm clouds are descending, a dark foreboding of what is to follow. In both instances, her story breaks into the dominant thread of ominous plotting. The time is just before Passover. The place is Bethany, right outside Jerusalem. Some of the religious leaders had just gathered in Jerusalem to begin plotting the death of Jesus.[2] But they are cautious in their plotting. Passover, a time to celebrate the liberation of God's people, is not the time to start trouble in an occupied territory. They know they need to watch . . . and wait . . . and bide their time for just the opportune moment. And then it comes, immediately after this woman's appearance. For Judas Iscariot, one of Jesus' own, immediately seeks them out, in order to betray Jesus.

She is a mystery, and she speaks not a word, but she is worthy of remembrance. Jesus said of her, "truly, I say to you, wherever the gospel is preached in the whole world, what she has done will be told in memory of her." But we have nearly forgotten her. Or remembered her primarily through Luke's version of the story, as a repentant sinner, who cried all over the feet of Jesus and dried them with her hair.[3] Who is this courageous woman, as she appears in Mark? And why does Jesus regard her actions with such significance that they are worthy of remembrance?

### HER IDENTITY

We do not know, of course, who she is. It might be helpful to say, first of all, who she is not. She is not Mary of Bethany, who anoints the feet of Jesus and dries them with her hair.[4] She is not the sinful woman of Luke's Gospel, who anoints the feet of Jesus early in his ministry, rather than just before the Passion. She is not Mary of Magdala, whom the Western tradition has described—inaccurately—as the "sinful woman," much forgiven, who anointed the feet of Jesus.[5] No, she is none of these.

But the mystery of her identity remains. Has she been healed by Jesus? Certainly, she has experienced his God-power in some significant way. Is she an outcast of some kind? Someone who has been profoundly welcomed by Jesus? Enough to allow her boldness to blossom? According to Mary Ann Tolbert, women tended to ignore "the social rules of modesty only if they were already among the 'shamed' (e.g. slaves, freed slaves, prostitutes, actresses) or were willing to be viewed that way."[6] Finally, it must be asked. Is she one of the women disciples, even an ideal disciple? According to Mark, she certainly understands who Jesus is and what true discipleship is all about. Somehow she has heard the word of God and understands what seems to be eluding the male disciples, that Jesus has come "not to be served but to serve, and to give his life as a ransom for many."[7] She perceives the darkness surrounding Jesus and pours out all that she has on him, as Jesus has done and will continue to do for us. Is she some combination of the above? We do not know.

But, we can be certain of this much. She has wealth. This perfumed oil is a luxury item, imported from the east, worth nearly a year's daily wages. She has compassion, enough to break open and pour out all this wealth—perhaps the sum total of her wealth—on Jesus. She has insight, enough to "see" the person of Jesus . . . Suffering Servant Messiah . . . and a man, in need of tenderness. She has courage, enough to break open all the rules of polite society. She has strength, enough to withstand the indignation—even rage—of the guests at the party. She has prophetic wisdom, enough to risk everything to anoint him "king." No wonder Jesus deems her worthy of remembrance!

## THE SIGNIFICANCE OF HER ACTIONS

She speaks not a word, but her actions reveal the God-given power that flows out of her. She stands tall, behind and above Jesus, who is seated at table. Confident and courageous, she pours out her resources, her very self, on Jesus. In doing so, she is like a prophet of old, anointing the kings of Israel.[8] And she does this, knowing what Peter and the others cannot yet accept, that this king is about to die.[9] In effect, she consecrates him for his mission. The symbols in her story reinforce this understanding. The breaking open of a vessel was a frequent symbol of death and destruction;[10] and, in Hellenistic times, such vessels were often left broken open in burial places.[11]

Artists seldom draw this picture. Rather, it is the sinful, repentant woman of Luke, at Jesus' feet, who has most often inspired Christian art. She is more in line with the cultural picture of women in the first century. And yet, the woman standing tall does appear in the Psalter of a Cistercian convent, painted about the year 1260. It is a picture of the Last Supper, with a woman in nun's garb, standing over and behind Jesus, pouring her precious ointment on his head.[12] There is also another woman, with long flowing hair, under the table, at Jesus' feet. Elisabeth Moltmann-Wendel suggests that this latter woman may have been a concession of the nuns to the tradition, while expressing, at the same time, the God-given power of woman to anoint a ruler, one who is about to give his life, as "a ransom for many." Maybe they even saw the Wisdom Woman of Proverbs in this woman, who proclaimed, "by me kings reign, and rulers decree what is just."[13]

Whoever she is, this woman "fits" in Mark's Gospel. For the Jesus of Mark's Gospel is very human, "down to earth" we might say. He is unafraid of touching and expressing his feelings. He mixes spittle and earth to heal a blind man. He makes sure that the daughter of Jairus has something to eat, immediately after raising her from the dead. He takes a child "in his arms" before offering the child as an illustration of receptivity toward himself. He is "distressed and agitated" on the eve of the Passion, in Gethsemane.

This Jesus of Mark's Gospel is even unafraid of breaking the chains of taboos by his touching. He breaks open the taboo about touching a leper, thus "making him clean." He breaks open the taboo about touching a dead body, when he takes the daughter of Jairus by the hand to raise her from the dead. He breaks open the taboo around menstruation as uncleanness by commending the woman with the flow of blood. She has "touched" him; but she is "daughter," a woman whose faith has made her well. In the same way, the woman-anointer not only breaks open the taboo that women do not barge into all-male dinner parties, but she breaks open the taboo that women do not presume to perform the prophetic rites of men. Jesus is in need; and she pours out all that she has to meet that need. She mirrors Jesus, who says to us, "Truly I tell you, wherever the good news is proclaimed in the whole world, what she has done will be told in remembrance of her."

## SOME RESOURCES

• • • • • • • • • • • • • • •

Fiorenza, Elisabeth Schüssler. *In Memory of Her: A Feminist Theological Reconstruction of Christian Origins.* New York: The Crossroad Publishing Company, 1985.

Grassi, Joseph A. *The Hidden Heroes of the Gospels: Female Counterparts of Jesus.* Collegeville, MN: The Liturgical Press, 1989.

Moltmann-Wendel, Elisabeth. "The Unknown Woman Who Anointed Jesus," pp. 92-104 in *The Women Around Jesus.* New York: The Crossroad Publishing Company, 1982.

Tolbert, Many Ann. "Mark" in *Women's Bible Commentary, Expanded Edition, with Apocrypha.* Ed. Carol A. Newsom and Sharon H. Ringe. Louisville, KY: Westminster John Knox Press, 1998.

Winter, Miriam Therese. *WomanWord: A Feminist Lectionary and Psalter, Women of the New Testament.* New York: The Crossroad Publishing Company, 1990.

Zimmer, Mary. *Sister Images: Guided Meditations from the Stories of Biblical Women.* Nashville, TN: Abingdon Press, 1993.

## NOTES

• • • • •

1. See Matthew 26:6-13.

2. Mark mentions chief priests and scribes; Matthew mentions chief priests and elders of the people, gathered in the palace of the high priest, Caiphas.

3. See Luke 7:36-50. This version takes the prophetic edge off the woman of Mark and Matthew, who courageously anointed Jesus on the head. Luke's purpose is different, highlighting a theme of forgiveness of sin; the woman in his story is also more in line with the cultural norm of subservient woman.

4. See John's version of the story, as recorded in John 12:1-8. This story, too, takes place in Bethany, but at the home of Lazarus, Martha, and Mary. It, too, is surrounded by plotting but takes place six days before the Passover.

5. In the Western tradition, Mary of Magdala became confused and lumped together with Mary of Bethany; they both became confused with the "sinful woman" of Luke. By the time of Pope Gregory the Great, in the sixth century, Mary of Magdala "became" this "sinful woman" rather than the "apostle to the apostles" of the Eastern tradition.

6. Mary Ann Tolbert, "Mark," in *Women's Bible Commentary, Expanded Edition*, edited by Carol A. Newsom and Sharon H. Ringe (Louisville, KY: Westminster John Knox Press, 1998), p. 352.

7.  See Mark 10:45, Jesus' most profound self understanding in this Gospel.

8.  See 1 Samuel 10:1, 16:13, for example.

9.  See Mark 8:31-34, 9:30-34, for example.

10. Joseph A. Grassi, *The Hidden Heroes of the Gospels* (Collegeville, MN: The Liturgical Press, 1989), p. 37, refers to Ecclesiastes 12:1-6 and Jeremiah 13:12-14; hereafter referred to as Grassi.

11. Grassi, p. 37, referring to M. Lagrange, *Evangile selon Sant Marc*, p. 367.

12. See Elisabeth Moltmann-Wendel, *The Women Around Jesus* (New York: The Crossroad Publishing Company, 1982), pp. 92 and 101.

13. See Proverbs 8:15.

# eight

Martha

# Our Commitment Is Mature and Lasting

*The cross is central to this worship. As people enter, they will hear "Tree of Life" and "Adoramus Te, Christe" being played. If possible flute and keyboard accompaniment will be helpful. People will receive a program with a prominent cross on the cover. Everyone will also be asked to fill out a name tag with a cross on it.*

*There will be a large cross in the center of the worship space, with some simple greenery (and flowers) near it. Otherwise, there will only be a lectern for the book.*

*Ministers:   leader, Martha, reader, cantor, and musicians*

*Materials:   large cross, lectern and scriptures, name tags, greenery and flowers*

## Introductory Rites

CALL TO WORSHIP                                              *Please stand*

Leader:     My tongue was all bound up,
            my speech uncertain and unsure.
            I stuttered and stumbled
            until Christ got hold of me.

| All: | Yes, I believe. |
| | I believe into Christ[1] who transforms; |
| | into Christ who changes everything. |

| Leader: | I still struggle . . . and stumble. |
| | It is slow, this business of transformation. |
| | But I keep on hearing the words of the Word become flesh, |
| | "Come, my beloved, talk to me, believe . . . and follow me." |

| All: | Yes, I believe. |
| | I believe into Christ who transforms, |
| | into Christ who changes everything. |

| Leader: | What words-become-flesh in us |
| | will be a sign of our believing? |
| | What words will we need to enflesh |
| | to set God's people free? |

| All: | O Christ, help us to believe, |
| | so that you-in-us can change everything, |
| | beginning with us. |

## OPENING HYMN
. . . . . . . . . . . .

"The Summons," text by John L. Bell, Iona Community, © 1987; tune is "Kelvingrove" (Scottish traditional), arr. by John L. Bell, Iona Community, © 1987, GIA Publications, Inc.

# Liturgy of the Word
. . . . . . . . . . . . . . . . . . . . . . . . . . . . . . . . . . . . . . . . . . .

DEUTERONOMY 6:4-9                                    *Please be seated*
. . . . . . . . . . . . . . . . . . .

PSALM 34
. . . . . . . .

"O Taste and See," text by Marty Haugen (based on Psalm 34), tune by Marty Haugen, GIA Publications, Inc., © 1993

GOSPEL: JOHN 11:1-44
. . . . . . . . . . . . . . . .

## REFLECTION (Martha)

Hello, everyone! My name is Martha! I can see by your knowing smiles and your nods that many of you know who I am! Some of you know me as strong, persistent, outspoken, and practical, a good and loyal friend. Yes, I often gave Jesus a place to lay his head in my home, right here in Bethany, whenever he came to Jerusalem. Of course, not everyone appreciates all my finer qualities, I will tell you! Well, I *am* the oldest in my family, sister to Mary and Lazarus.[2] And you know how it can be with the oldest, always taking charge. Bossy, *some* might say. Lazarus is the youngest, and he's such a gentle man. Mary's gentle, too, a dreamer, the one who can spend hours off by herself, in silence. Well, I do have my own ways of being with God, but sometimes I really wish I could sit still as long as Mary does. Maybe some of you understand . . . even identify with me. Maybe others of you are annoyed with me because I have come to be known as the complainer.[3] Well, I can only say this—for the moment. As different as we were, Jesus loved us unconditionally. He delighted in each of us—Mary, Lazarus, and me. He was at home with us, and we were at home with him.

But, this story is not about us. It's about Jesus. And our relationship with Jesus. How we came to know him, really *know* him, and believe in him, as Christ, the Son of God. How we allowed that knowing to change us, transform us into true disciples, his beloved.

So, let me tell you about the time I was finally able to put into words what my whole being had come to believe. I was about to say, "It began like this. My beloved brother took sick, and quickly became deathly ill." But, no, it *really* began long before that day.

It began with all those conversations on into the night. About the time that Jesus healed the man who had been ill for thirty-eight years, lying helplessly by the pool of the Sheep Gate. . . . Or about the time that he healed the man born blind. At times like this, his face became an open book. Revealing flashes of anger at religious leaders, who put more stock in the letter of Sabbath law than the needs of broken people. Or, revealing gut-wrenching compassion for anyone paralyzed, stuck in life, whether in body or in spirit. At any rate, little by little, I began to see for myself, not unlike that man born blind. Jesus was the one we'd all been waiting for! He was more than a prophet, more than God's messenger. He was *filled* with God's life! And I knew that *nothing* could stop that irrepressible flow of life, no matter what.

So, of course, when Lazarus became so very sick, Mary and I urgently sent the message, "Come! Quickly!" But he didn't come . . . not right away. Lazarus died. And we had to bury him immediately, for it is our custom. Finally, I heard that Jesus was near our home. Finally! Four days later! I didn't wait for him to walk through our door. Out I went, to grieve, to give him a piece of my mind . . . and to put my trust in him, one more time, "even now," even now. But, what was this I saw in his face? Certainly tenderness, even profound love . . . for me, for Lazarus, for Mary. But, there was something more. He searched out my face, my heart, my very being. For understanding? For total trust in him? Could I believe, in him, even without knowing the whole picture, the reason for his delay? Could I trust in his enduring love for me, for us all? "Yes!" The words tumbled out of my depths. "You are the Messiah, the Son of God." Gratitude spread over that beautiful face, companion to the gut-wrenching sadness that remained.

You know the rest of the story. Well, some of it, anyway. Lazarus was raised from the dead. And, it was the beginning of the end for Jesus. Or, should I say it was the near-beginning of the "hour" he so often talked about. *(Pause, continue reflectively.)*

But even I had no idea what that "hour" would cost. Or that I, like the others, would be marked forever by the shattering wound of that Friday. . . . But evening came, the evening of "the first day of the week."[4] And Jesus, forever scarred himself . . . by love . . . broke through all the bolted doors of fear. It was true! Love is always the final word! *(Pause)* I would need to remember that time and time again. For I became leader of my house church.[5] It's a natural. My gifts for hospitality are legendary! I *always* knew how to set quite a table! Only this time, it's the Table of the Lord. As for preaching, I never was at a loss for words. Only now, the force of love, truth, and eternal life is behind them. And that makes all the difference! For it seems that my leadership creates quite a stir, among some people, at least. "How can a woman be doing all that," some want to know! How, indeed! Only by knowing . . . and following Jesus . . . the Messiah, the Son of God. Wherever he leads, from death to new life. Do you believe?

## MUSICAL RESPONSE

"Digo 'Sí,' Señor/ I Say 'Yes,' Lord," text and tune by Donna Peña, with tune arrangement by Marty Haugen, GIA Publications, Inc., © 1989.

# Liturgy of Mature Faith Commitment

## INTRODUCTION *(Martha)*

Jesus asked me, "Do you believe?" He did not mean, "Do you believe in me as an article of faith, in an abstract way?" No, he meant, "Do you *know* me? With your heart, your soul, and all your might?" He meant, "Will you follow me? Will you let me make all the difference in your life, transform your very being?" And I said "Yes," with everything in me.

Now I invite you to respond to the following questions, by saying, "Yes, I am," echoing Jesus the Christ. For he was the very one who proclaimed, "I am the resurrection and the life," or simply, "I am."

Martha:    Are you desiring and willing to believe in Christ, to really know him?

Response:  Yes, I am.

Martha:    Are you desiring and willing to become one with Jesus, the Christ, and to love the people Jesus loves?

Response:  Yes, I am.

Martha:    Are you desiring and willing to follow wherever Christ leads you, even to the cross?

Response:  Yes, I am.

Martha:    Are you desiring and willing to embrace life fully, in all its sorrow and all its joy?

Response:  Yes, I am.

Martha:    Are you desiring and willing to help unbind and set God's people free?

Response:  Yes, I am.

## INVITATION TO THE CROSS[6]

Martha:    I invite you now to come to the cross, two by two, so that you might be blessed with the sign of the cross on your forehead, eyes, ears, hands, and feet. These are the words you will hear: _____, receive the cross on your

---

forehead, your eyes, your ears, your hands, and your feet (*as each part of your body is signed*). It is Christ who strengthens you with this sign of his love. Learn to know, see, hear, touch, follow, and become Christ more fully.

Response:    Amen! Yes, let it be!

Martha:    The first pair will be blessed by the leader and myself. In turn, you will bless the two behind you, while the leader and I recite the words of the blessing. The signing will continue in this way.

## MUSIC DURING THE RITUAL

"Tree of Life," sung once with all verses, text by Marty Haugen, tune adapted from "Thomas" by Marty Haugen, GIA Publications, © 1984.

or

"Tree of Life," sung with "Adoramus Te Christe" (text is an antiphon from the Good Friday Liturgy, "We adore you, O Christ, and we bless you, because by your holy cross you have redeemed the world"), tune by Marty Haugen, GIA Publications, Inc., © 1984.

or

"If You Believe and I Believe," text is Zimbabwean traditional, tune is Zimbabwean traditional, adapted from English traditional, arr. by John L. Bell, Iona Community, GIA Publications, Inc., © 1991.

# Closing Rites

BLESSING                                                              *Please stand*

Leader:    Go forth in the life of God, our Creator.
           "For God so loved the world that he gave his only Son,
           so that everyone who believes in him many not perish
           but may have eternal life."[7]

All:       "In the cross of Christ, our glory,
           Christ, our story, Christ, our song."[8]

Leader:    Go forth in the love of Christ, our Redeemer,
           "who, though he was in the form of God,

did not regard equality with God as something to be
exploited."9

All: "In the cross of Christ, our glory,
    Christ, our story, Christ, our song."

Leader: Go forth in the truth of Christ's Spirit outpoured.
    For "when the Spirit of truth comes,
    he will guide you into all the truth."10

All: "In the cross of Christ, our glory,
    Christ, our story, Christ, our song."

## CLOSING HYMN
● ● ● ● ● ● ● ● ● ● ● ●

"You Are the Voice," text and tune by David Haas, GIA Publications, Inc., © 1987.

## NOTES
● ● ● ● ●

1. The writer of John's Gospel uses a Greek construction thirty-six times that is not found elsewhere in Greek literature: *pisteuein eis*, followed by a noun in the accusative case, which literally means "to believe into." In John's Gospel, such "believing into" Jesus, the Christ, means a profound kind of knowing, that of a lover or close friend. See Sandra M. Schneiders, *Written That You May Believe: Encountering Jesus in the Fourth Gospel* (New York: The Crossroad Publishing Company, A Herder & Herder Book, 1999), pp. 51-53; hereafter referred to as Schneiders.

2. There is nothing I have seen to suggest this, other than her personality and the fact that Luke says in his Martha/Mary story, "a woman named Martha welcomed him [Jesus] *into her home*" (my emphasis, see Luke 10:38). So, it's possible that she was the oldest. It must also be noted that the Bethany in Luke's Gospel is in Galilee, not the same Bethany of John's Gospel, that is right outside Jerusalem.

3. This sentence reflects the image of Martha as found in Luke 10:38-42. But, Barbara J. Reid in her *Choosing the Better Part?: Women in the Gospel of Luke* (Collegeville, MN: The Liturgical Press, 1996), unravels and reconstructs the Lucan story with new understandings. As she points out, Luke might well be reflecting the conflict going on in the community of the 80s about the *diakonia* (meaning service) of women, rather than a story in the ministry of Jesus. This story takes place at the home (house church?) of Martha; Martha was distracted by "many tasks," none of which mention fussing in the kitchen. Martha was pitted against Mary, a likely scenario in the late first century, with "sisters" disagreeing about the role of women in the church. And, her "worry and distraction" have the connotation in Greek of a major disturbance, going outside the confines of the home.

4.   See John 20:19-23.

5.   This follows from the suggestions of Barbara E. Reid in *Choosing the Better Part?: Women in the Gospel of Luke.* See the companion information on Martha for more details.

6.   This ritual is taken from the ritual of "Acceptance Into the Order of Catechumens." While it is regarded in the church as an initial step toward full initiation, it is used here as a sign of embracing the fullness of Christian life, the paschal mystery of the cross.

7.   See John 3:16.

8.   These are the words of one of the refrains offered in the Ritual of "Acceptance Into the Order of Catechumens."

9.   See Philippians 2:6.

10.  See John 16:13a.

# Martha: Unbind Her and Let Her Go Free

"Unbind her and let her go free!" This paraphrase of Jesus' words to the community about Lazarus certainly applies to Martha today. She has been bound up by the story in Luke's Gospel (Luke 10:38-42) and the popular perception of her as a whiney complainer. Few people recognize Martha as the strong woman of faith and beloved friend of Jesus in John's Gospel, who makes the ultimate confession of faith that we normally associate with Peter.[1] Even fewer know the medieval legends of the strong, spiritually mature Martha who overcomes the dragon—symbol of all evil—by binding it up, rather than destroying it. In doing so, she leaves open the ultimate possibility of redemption. Now this is a Martha worth liberating!

We all know the Martha of Luke's Gospel. Busy about many things. Anxious. Complaining to Jesus that her "sister" doesn't help out. Seemingly rebuked by Jesus, "Martha, Martha. . . ." This is the woman that so many others can identify with: a woman whose work is never done, a woman who never seems to get enough help, a woman who knows what has to be done and does it. And yet, in the identification, one is left with an uneasy, nagging question. Does Jesus disapprove of her . . . of me?

Some scholars are now questioning Luke's reputation of being "favorable" toward women. Indeed, there is the growing recognition that although Luke tells numerous stories of women, the women are increasingly passive, even silenced, over the span of his two-volume work, The Gospel of Luke and The Acts of the Apostles. According to Joseph Grassi, Luke emphasizes the role of Peter and The Twelve, sometimes over and against women, in order to give official credibility to some essential beliefs about Jesus (i.e., his physical body and the mystery of a powerless, Suffering Messiah).[2] Jane Schaberg opens her commentary on Luke's Gospel with a warning. Although "this Gospel highlights women as included among the followers of Jesus, subjects of his teaching and objects of his healing, it deftly portrays them as models of subordinate service, excluded from the power center of the movement and from significant responsibilities."[3] And Elisabeth Schüssler Fiorenza is the first to suggest that the Lucan Martha suffers from the conflict going on in the community over the roles of women in house churches, rather than from the disapproval of Jesus.[4] But it is Barbara E. Reid who does Martha—and us—a great service in her penetrating gaze upon the Lucan Martha.[5] Let's take a closer look.

Barbara Reid takes the passage (Luke 10:38-42) seriously, with all its tensions. In the end, she concludes that the tension is really about Martha's *diakonia*, or service, mentioned twice in verse 40.[6] But she begins by raising the questions imbedded in the passage. Why are action and contemplation set in opposition to one another? Especially when Luke consistently proclaims that the action of Jesus comes out of prayer? Why are the sisters set in opposition to one another? Why does Jesus appear to reprimand Martha's service, when he himself serves, often and openly? Why does the Lucan Jesus, ordinarily so compassionate, seem to have no compassion for Martha? Is it Martha's attitude of "anxiety" that is the problem (as some suggest, who try to "rescue" Jesus from seeming harshness)? And yet, elsewhere, the Lucan Jesus is concerned about anxiety over the pleasures of this world that choke the word's growth (8:14) or worries over daily life (21:22, 34). Martha's "anxiety" is not of that variety; hers has to do with "much serving." (By the way, note that *nothing* is said about fussing in the kitchen or preparing a meal, as is often presumed to be the case.) The only plausible conclusion for Barbara Reid, as for Elisabeth Schüssler Fiorenza, is that this story reveals tension—even between "sisters"—regarding women's service in the early Christian communities.[7]

And tension there was! According to Schaberg, "*diakonia* became a technical term referring to eucharistic table service, proclamation, and ecclesial leadership."[8] In some communities, especially in some of the

Pauline communities, this *diakonia* of women was welcomed.[9] But, by the end of the first century, as the writer(s) of letters to Timothy (1 Timothy 2:11-15) and Titus (2:3-5) reveal, women are to be silent! And, a woman's place is in the home! In fact, a number of scholars now believe that Paul's First Letter to the Corinthians, written in the early 50s, was altered by a later copyist, to reflect this later silencing of women.[10] In order to drive home her point, that women's ecclesial ministry is the issue here, Reid notes that the Greek verb *"thorybazo"* (worried) is only found here (verse 41) in the New Testament. When the noun form is used elsewhere, it is found in the context of a disturbance made by a crowd.[11] Martha's *diakonia* was creating quite a stir! At least, that's how Luke saw it.

In John's Gospel, Martha is portrayed in a very different light. Oh, she is still strong and still vocal. But, she fits into a gospel of strong, vocal women, like the Samaritan Woman, and Mary of Magdala, first apostle of the Easter Gospel. And she is the model disciple, "loved by Jesus" (John 11:5, similar to "the one whom Jesus loved"[12]), who believes! She makes the ultimate faith statement of the entire gospel, that Jesus is "the Messiah, the Son of God." And she *knows* that this believing gives life! In her very person, then, she fulfills the entire purpose of the evangelist in writing this gospel: "so that you may come to believe that Jesus is the Messiah, the Son of God, and that through this believing you may have life in his name."[13]

According to Sandra Schneiders, this story of Martha and the "raising of Lazarus" is the Fourth Gospel in miniature: "that Jesus came to give divine life in all its fullness to those who believe in him."[14] If that is so, how is the death of believers to be understood?[15]Martha wrestled with that question. The Johannine community wrestled with that question, as do we. Is Jesus absent? As he appeared to be, for Martha and Mary? Is death for real? Or is Lazarus merely asleep? Oh, "Lazarus is dead," all right; death is brutally real. And Martha, ever practical, knew that "already there is a stench," after four days in the tomb. Does Jesus care? He delays, for he understands the ultimate purpose of his mission, which is "for God's glory." (Ironically, it is this very raising of Lazarus which sets in motion his "hour," the "glory of God," resurrection out of death. Some of the religious leaders now find Jesus "too much" and immediately plot his death.) But he also weeps, along with Mary and "the Jews who came with her." Suffering is appropriate, but despair is not. For, in Jesus, death "finally serves the purpose of God, which is to bring all believers into union with God in Jesus."[16] And Martha believes, a hard won believing. She believes in Jesus, "even now." She is the true disciple, speaking for all true disciples, who have come to know the unconquerable, unquenchable force of eternal life in Jesus. Jesus may be physically absent, but his abiding and intimate presence is very real, now and forever. Death is painfully powerful; but in Jesus, death never has the last word.

In the tradition, especially during the Middle Ages, this believing strength of Martha ultimately became symbolized in her subduing of the dragon, symbol of chaos and evil. It may seem odd, at first glance, that a strong woman becomes an important symbol during the Middle Ages. True enough, men were still dominant. In the fourteenth century, Catherine of Siena is reported to have complained to God about being sent on a mission more appropriately done by a man. And yet, she was a diplomat, sought out for her skill, and the confidante of two popes. Two centuries earlier, Hildegard of Bingen had been invited on preaching tours by bishops of the Rhine Valley, when she was in her sixties. From the twelfth century onward, change was in the air: the rise of cities and a money economy, altered family systems with different sets of needs. Some women began to advocate for social reform; and religious groups of women mushroomed around active Christian love of neighbor. Martha, the active one, became a symbol for a number of these groups. As early as 1300, Meister Eckhart, mystic and Dominican monk, praised Martha's mature faith. "What a wondrous involvement both outwardly and inwardly: understanding and being understood; seeing and being seen; holding and being held; that is the last stage where the Spirit perseveres in rest, united to beloved eternity."[17] The passive woman of old was replaced by this active, mature Martha.

Indeed, this "new Martha met the needs of women who dissociated themselves from the old orders and looked for a new self-understanding."[18] She was found in legends. She was found in art. In the early Middle Ages, a legend developed in southern France around Mary (Magdalene, mistakenly presumed to be Mary of Bethany), Martha, and Lazarus. They are driven out of Palestine, put on a raft, and arrive in southern France. In time, Martha became a strong, independent woman, one to be emulated. She preaches, heals, and raises a person from the dead.[19] Giovanni di Milano painted her in a side chapel of Santa Croce in Florence (1336) as the host at Bethany, radiating an inner light.[20] In another portrait, on another altar, she stands alongside Lazarus, now a bishop, "in beautiful tranquility and spiritual sovereignty."[21] In yet another, by the Dominican Fra Angelico, she prays, just outside Gethsemane, the only disciple to mirror the actions of Jesus.[22] Now her action is a prayerful "watching" with Jesus. She is the "great mother," "embodiment of the mature, powerful, creative woman who fulfils herself and makes her own contribution, who calls forth the wonderment of the male."[23] Finally, she is artistically found defeating the dragon, first in southern France in the fourteenth century, then in northern Italy and southern Germany over the next two centuries. She is confident, even proud, and self-assured. "In one hand she usually holds a pitcher and a holy water sprinkler or a cross, with which she has bound the dragon. In the other hand she is holding her girdle, the symbol of purity, with which she has fettered him."[24] She is the counterpart of the male hero, St. George. But, instead of slaying the dragon, she subdues evil with the power of holy water and the purity of her girdle, leaving open the possibility of transformation. She proclaims her belief in "I am the resurrection and the life" in a whole new way. But the legend of St. George, child of a male church, has prevailed over the woman Martha.

Feminist scholars today are calling Martha forth from the tomb of her whiney, complaining image, an image that is worth less than Mary's contemplation. They are calling forth the church to unbind her and let her go free. And, in the process, they are calling forth each and every one of us to believe. To become—like Martha—strong, creative, faith-filled believers in(to) Jesus, the Resurrection and the Life.

## SOME RESOURCES

Brown, Raymond E., S.S. *The Anchor Bible. The Gospel According to John (I-XII)*. Garden City, NY: Doubleday & Company, 1966.

Fiorenza, Elisabeth Schüssler. "A Feminist Critical Interpretation for Liberation: Martha and Mary: Luke 10:38-42," *Religion & Intellectual Life* 3 (1986) 21-36.

Grassi, Joseph A. *The Hidden Heroes of the Gospels: Female Counterparts of Jesus*. Collegeville, MN: The Liturgical Press, 1989.

McKenna, Megan. *Leave Her Alone*. Maryknoll, NY: Orbis Books, 2000.

Moltmann-Wendel, Elisabeth. *The Women Around Jesus*. New York: The Crossroad Publishing Company, 1982.

O'Day, Gail R. "John," in *Women's Bible Commentary, Expanded Edition, with Apocrypha*. Editors Carol A. Newsom and Sharon H. Ringe. Louisville, KY: Westminster John Knox Press, 1998, pp. 381-393.

Reid, Barbara E. *Choosing the Better Part?: Women in the Gospel of Luke*. Collegeville, MN: A Michael Glazier Book by The Liturgical Press, 1996.

Schaberg, Jane. "Luke," in *Women's Bible Commentary, Expanded Edition, with Apocrypha*. Editors Carol A. Newsom and Sharon H. Ringe. Louisville, KY: Westminster John Knox Press, 1998, pp. 363-380.

Schneiders, Sandra M. *Written That You May Believe: Encountering Jesus in the Fourth Gospel*. New York: A Herder & Herder Book by The Crossroad Publishing Company, 1999.

Winter, Miriam Therese. *WomanWord: A Feminist Lectionary and Psalter, Women of the New Testament*. New York: The Crossroad Publishing Company, 1990.

Zimmer, Mary. *Sister Images: Guided Meditations from the Stories of Biblical Women*. Nashville: Abingdon Press, 1993.

## NOTES

• • • • •

1.   See Mark 8:27-30 // Matthew 16:13-20 // Luke 9:18-21.

2.   See Joseph A. Grassi, *The Hidden Heroes of the Gospels: Female Counterparts of Jesus* (Collegeville, MN: The Liturgical Press, 1989), pp. 83-112.

3.   Jane Schaberg, "Luke," in *Women's Bible Commentary, Expanded Edition, with Apocrypha*. Editors Carol A. Newsom and Sharon H. Ringe (Louisville, KY: Westminster John Knox Press, 1998), p. 363; hereafter referred to as Schaberg.

4.   Elisabeth Schüssler Fiorenza, "A Feminist Critical Interpretation for Liberation: Martha and Mary: Luke 10:38-42," *Religion & Intellectual Life* 3 (1986) 21-36.

5.   See Barbara E. Reid, *Choosing the Better Part?: Women in the Gospel of Luke* (Collegeville, MN: The Liturgical Press, 1996), pp. 144-162; hereafter referred to as Reid.

6.   The most accurate translation of verse 40 would be: Martha, burdened with much serving, came to him and said, "Lord, do you not care that my sister has left me by myself to do the serving? Tell her to help me." See Reid, p. 144.

7.   This would explain why Martha and Mary are pitted against one another. It is also worth noting that Martha does not refer to Mary by name in verse 40, when she asks for help; Christian women, especially those in ecclesial service, were sometimes called "sisters."

8.   Schaberg, p. 377.

9.   See, for example, Romans 16:1-7. In Philippians 4:2-3, Paul acknowledges the crucial leadership of Euodia and Syntyche, whom he regards as coworkers. See more on Prisca (Priscilla) in Acts 18:1-4, 24-26; 1 Corinthians 16:19; and 2 Timothy 4:19.

10. See 1 Corinthians 11:34-35.

11. Reid, p. 158.

12. See references to the "beloved disciple" in John 13:23; 19:26; 20:2; 21:7, 20. This disciple's believing is based upon intimate knowing of Jesus.

13. See Martha's statement in John 11:27 reflected in the evangelist's purpose in John 20:31 (the last verse of the original Gospel, since chapter 21 was added later).

14. Sandra M. Schneiders, *Written That You May Believe: Encountering Jesus in the Fourth Gospel* (New York: A Herder & Herder Book by The Crossroad Publishing Company, 1999), p. 153; hereafter referred to as Schneiders. She refers to the following passages in John: 1:12, 3:16, 5:24, 6:50-51, 10:10, among others.

15. Schneiders maintains that this question is the basis for the story of the "raising of Lazarus." See p. 152.

16. Schneiders, p. 156.

17. Elisabeth Moltmann-Wendel, *The Women Around Jesus* (New York: The Crossroad Publishing Company, 1982).

18. Ibid., p. 34.

19. Ibid., p. 43.

20. Ibid., p. 35.

21. Ibid.

22. Ibid., pp. 30, 37-38.

23. Ibid., p. 37.

24. Ibid., p. 42.

*nine*

Ruth and Naomi

# Sharing Wisdom Across Generations Gives Life

*The worship space is set up ideally so that people can face one another. The central focus of the space is a large table with one candle, a simple harvest decoration, and a simple but beautiful basket, large enough to hold a note card from everyone present. On one side of the table is a lectern, on which is placed the Story of Ruth and Naomi. The presider and two other people, the two voices, will sit with the people, next to the lectern. People are greeted as they enter and given a program, a note card, and a pencil.*

*This liturgy might be used with any intergenerational gathering, like an intergenerational faith formation group, a mother/daughter event, or any other faith event that cuts across age lines.*

Ministers:   *leader, two voices, cantor, and musicians*

Materials:   *large table, candle, harvest decoration, basket, note cards, pencils*

## Introductory Rites

*The presider greets everyone in these or similar words:*

People of all ages, from youth to elderly, have wisdom to share. Today we celebrate the wisdom gained from our life choices as we focus on two women—a mother-in-law and daughter-in-law—who chose abiding friendship and life. So, now, we begin our celebration by greeting one another, honoring the wisdom in each of us.

## GATHERING HYMN
. . . . . . . . . . . . . . .

"O Praise God All You Nations" ("Laudate Omnes Gentes"), The Iona Community, GIA Publications, Inc., agent, music © 1995.

or

"Raise a Song of Gladness" ("Jubilate, Servite"), text based upon Psalm 100, Taize Community, Les Presses de Taize, GIA Publications, Inc., ©1978, tune by Jacques Berthier © 1979.

*These are simple hymns, each of which can be sung in a round. It is a good gathering exercise to have the song leader introduce the song and rehearse it with each half of the room. It sets the tone, that God is present in all people of all ages at all times. And that is real cause for celebration. People are invited to stand when it is time to begin.*

## OPENING BLESSING                                    *Please stand*
. . . . . . . . . . . . . . .

*(the two sides of the assembly face each another)*

Leader:      We bless God, God's people, and God's good earth, sea,
             and sky.

Right side: We bless God and we bless you, God's people.

Left side:   We bless God and we bless you, God's people.

All:          We bless all of creation, God's good earth, sea, and sky.

# Liturgy of the Word
. . . . . . . . . . . . . . . . . . . . . . . . . . . . . . . . . . . . . . . . . . . . . . . . . . .

## A WRITING BASED ON THE BOOK OF RUTH (*in two voices*)
. . . . . . . . . . . . . . . . . . . . . . . . . . . . . . . . . . . . . . . . . . . . . . . . . .

*Voice 1:*

They were at a crossroads,
two women—alone: together.

The older woman was well acquainted with grief . . .
the loss of a husband
and their two sons,
the only children of her womb.

The dark cloud of mourning overshadowed her,
shrouding her wisdom in fear, depression, and utter resignation.
"Call me no longer Naomi"—
which means pleasant.
No, "call me Mara"—
which means bitter—
"because the hand of the Lord has turned against me."

At an earlier crossroads,
thrust from their homes by famine,
this now emptied family
had left the "House of Bread," Bethlehem,
for the promise of bread in Moab.
But now . . .

finally . . .
having heard that God "had considered" her people,
Naomi was heading home.

With nothing to offer her daughter-in-law
—or so she thought—
no hope of another husband,
and *certainly* no hope of a child,
Naomi was adamant.
Ruth was to return to the Moabites,
"to her people and to her gods."

*Voice 2:*

But the younger woman
refused to leave her. . . .
Insisted on
seeing what was not yet there . . .
persisted in
drawing possibilities out of the older one,
like drawing water out of her "Wisdom Well."

She covenanted . . .
"Wherever you go, I will go" . . .
cleaving to Naomi . . . and an eagle-winged God.

---

And they conspired. . . .
Inspired . . .
by the God
who would satisfy every hunger, with some left over,
and forge an indelible bond
between young woman, foreigner, and older woman, wise.

*Voice 1:*

The older woman remembered
love . . .
the ways of her people . . .
the kind beauty of Ruth . . .
"a kinsman on her husband's side,
a prominent rich man," a just man named Boaz
who *might* serve as redeemer.

*Voice 2:*

They had arrived in Bethlehem at harvest time,
and the harvest was bountiful that year.
For seed was harvested
by Ruth,
enough to feed them both,
and more, much more . . .
compassionate, considerate, covenant love
and a son named Obed.

Yes.
Boaz claimed Ruth as his wife,
buoyed by the people-blessing at the village gate,
"May the Lord make the woman who is coming into your house
like Rachel and Leah,
who together built up the house of Israel."

*Voice 1:*

But it was Naomi
who was blest,
proclaimed the women.
For God "has not left [her] this day
without next-of-kin."
Indeed . . .
Obed "became the father of Jesse,
the father of David," the king of Israel.

And in the fullness of time
it was said by the evangelist Matthew
that Boaz was "the father of Obed by Ruth,
and Obed the father of Jesse,
and Jesse the father of King David."
And after another twenty-eight generations—or so it was said—
Joseph was "the husband of Mary,
of whom Jesus was born,
who is called the Messiah."

*Voice 2:*

Whose story is this?
Naomi's—Wisdom Well *finally* gushing forth in the wilderness?
Ruth's—Outsider, alien, foreigner embodying adopted Yahweh God?
The people's?
Remembering and celebrating *why* God had set them free?
Or was it David's—a "shoot" sprouting from the root of Jesse,
burrowed deep into rich soil, producing monarchy and Messiah?
Or is it ours, as well?
A story of relationship, of surprising God companionship,
of Wisdom pitching a tent in every generation
and barrenness giving birth,
of choices made at the crossroads of life.

## MUSICAL REFLECTION

"Wherever You Go" (text based upon Ruth 1:16-17), text and tune by
Gregory Norbet, The Benedictine Foundation of the State of Vermont,
Inc., © 1972, 1980. *Everyone is invited to join in singing this hymn.*

# A Ritual of Thanking and Blessing

## PREPARATION

Leader:     People matter. In good times and in bad. In making choic-
            es. In loss and the movement from emptiness to fullness. In
            "returning" home, to God, to life. In handing on what mat-
            ters most. Seemingly insignificant people can change us—
            or an entire nation—by their integrity. And age does not

seem to matter. It *can* be—as it was with Ruth—a young person, even an "outsider." But one willing to take unconditionally loving risks for the sake of life. Or, it *can* be—as it was with Naomi—an older woman, able to draw nearly forgotten wisdom out of that deep well of life experience.

I invite you now to think of someone—of any age—who has deeply affected your life. Someone living or dead. Someone from scripture or someone you know well in person. A grandparent or grandchild. A significant other in the broadest sense of that word. What might you say to thank that person? Consider this question, as you listen to this brief letter in response.

*(The following letter is given as an example.)*

*Voice 1:*

Dear Ruth,

I have read your story several times now, and each time I find something new. I have come to appreciate and admire you so much. Your willingness to take enormous risks . . . some might say leaps of faith. To marry someone outside your faith tradition and culture in the first place and then travel to an unknown land with someone who said she could offer you nothing. And, oh, how you love! In the way that God loves, without judgment, without condition, without looking for something in return. You love just because you cannot help it.

And most recently, I have come to admire the way you work within a system but push out the boundaries of that system. Let me say a little more about that.

*Voice 2:*

It is only most recently that I have come to see how much dignity you claim for yourself as you work within a man's world. Why is that important to me? Because the church I love is still in many ways a man's world. And I am passionate about lifting up the dignity of women within it, so that women and men can truly see each other as equal partners.

Just think about the life that can burst forth from *that* truth! For I truly believe that God's Spirit is stirring us, moving us in that direction.

And yet, at times, I get discouraged, like so many others. But you, Ruth, give me hope. I see in you a steadfast clinging to the God who frees us. I sense from you a faith that entrusts yourself to this God and then acts with wisdom and courage, creativity and even some good plotting on occasion to make sure that your dignity and that of your mother-in-law are honored. You are a beacon of hope all the way from ancient Israel to the edge of the twenty-first century.

Sincerely,

[Name]

## THE RITUAL

. . . . . . . . . .

*Presider:*    Take a moment now to write down on your card the name of your significant person. In a *very* brief note, thank that person for what matters most to you. Later, you might want to write a letter to that person, even if she or he is deceased. Then, as you are ready, please bring your card forward and place it is the basket for a blessing.

*The leader takes the basket off the table and holds it reverently as people come forward. At this time, the music begins gently. Everyone is invited to join in the refrain.*

## MUSIC

. . . . .

"Ubi Caritas" (text based on 1 Cor 13:2-8, "Where charity and love are found, God is there"), Taize Community, 1978; tune by Jacques Berthier, Les Presses de Taize, GIA Publications, Inc., © 1979.

*If needed, continue with the following:*

"Magnificat," text based on Luke 1:46-55; text and tune by David Haas, GIA Publications, Inc., © 1990.

## NAMING

. . . . . . .

*The leader lifts up the basket, inviting people to name aloud the person they are thanking.*

## BLESSING

*The leader then invites everyone to extend an arm in blessing and to pray together:*

God, beyond all names, we bless and honor you.
God, beyond all generations, we bless and praise you.
God, beyond all love, we bless and thank you
for these companions on our journey,
bread for our bodies,
healing for our souls. Amen.

# Closing Rites

## SENDING FORTH PRAYER                    *Please stand*

*The leader invites everyone to pray:*

Wherever we go, may we honor, praise, and thank God.
Wherever we go, may we honor our significant others.
Wherever we go, may we become a living Word of Wisdom,
to nourish and sustain, disturb and comfort all who pass our way.
Amen! Yes, let it be!

## CLOSING HYMN

"God, Beyond All Names," Bernadette Farrell. Published by OCP Publications, © 1990. All rights reserved.

# The Book of Ruth, The Story of Ruth, and Her Significance Today

In the Hebrew Scripture, the Book of Ruth is to be found in the Writings (after the Torah and the Prophets). It is read in the synagogue on the festival of Shavuot, which commemorates the giving of the Torah (the Five Books of Moses or the first five Books of the Hebrew Scripture). Christians place it between the Books of Judges and Samuel, among the historical books of the Bible. At first glance, it seems to be one family's movement from famine, exile, barrenness, and loss to a homecoming more abundant than anyone could have possibly imagined. And, it has become widely known as a story of profound, abiding friendship. But its charm may be deceptive, for this small book probes the meaning of human life on many levels.

## RUTH'S STORY . . .

First, though, let's look at the story itself. It takes place in the time of the Judges. The people of Israel have settled in the Promised Land but there is no kingdom yet. There is famine in the land of Israel, and "a certain man of Bethlehem in Judah went to live in the country of Moab, he and his wife and two sons" (Ruth 1:1). The man is Elimelech, his wife is Naomi, and his sons are Mahlon and Chilion. The sons marry Moabite women, named Ruth and Orpah. But time is not good to them; loss builds upon loss, as first Naomi's husband dies, and then both her sons. As she puts it, her name has been changed from Naomi, which means "pleasant," to Mara, which means "bitter." When she finally hears that the famine has ended, she determines to head back home; and she insists that her two daughters-in-law return to *their* gods and *their* people, so that they might marry again and find security. Orpah does as she is told, but Ruth will *not* go back; she will not leave Naomi. We hear from her some of the most stirring words of scripture, words that echo the God she insists on adopting as her own, "Where you go, I will go; where you lodge, I will lodge; your people shall be my people . . ." (Ruth 1:16). Together they head for Bethlehem, two women alone, one in deep grief. They arrive there at the time of the barley harvest, and Ruth sets about the work of feeding them by gleaning grain in the field. It so happens that she comes "to the part of the field belonging to Boaz, who was from the family of Elimelech" (Ruth 2:3). Now Naomi becomes aware that Boaz is protecting Ruth, and she begins to return to life, to conspire with Ruth. She comes up with a plan, customary among her people, for the next of kin to her dead husband to claim Ruth as his wife.[1] The plan succeeds. For Boaz is a kind and just man, deeply moved by Ruth's compassionate care for Naomi and her unerring trust in the God of Israel. The extra seed he has given Ruth in the field becomes symbolic of the seed he will give her in marriage. Indeed, they are married, but not before they are blessed by the people at the town gate, "May the Lord make the woman who is coming into your house like Rachel and Leah, who together built up the house of Israel" (Ruth 4:11). Their son is named Obed, who fills Naomi's emptiness. And we know what they cannot yet know, that Obed "became the father of Jesse, the father of

David" (Ruth 4:17). Furthermore, in the Gospel of Matthew, Ruth is one of five courageous women named in the lengthy—and otherwise male—genealogy of Jesus, the Messiah.

## AND OURS
· · · · · · · · ·

Surely Ruth's journey sounds familiar. Surely her story draws deeply from the well of our own life experience. Indeed, the authors of *Reading Ruth: Contemporary Women Reclaim a Sacred Story,*[2] probe the universal human themes in her story, gleaning some wisdom for us all.

First of all, this is a story of deep and abiding friendship—with all its ups and downs, its ebb and flow, its initiation first by one and then by the other, its fidelity in the midst of life's struggles, and its ability to thread a way between dependence and independence. Ruth's generosity overflows all bounds of obligation, enough to prime Naomi's pump, enough to draw life out of a woman withered by suffering and loss.

But it is even more. It is about God and us, about the nature of God and God's friendship with us. Such friendship has traditionally been called *"chesed"* or "loving kindness," an unconditional "I am with you, I am for you." Today, theologian Sallie McFague says that God is like a friend, who chooses us constantly, is vulnerable in the process, offers us unconditional love and acceptance, and is with us and for us.[3] What does it take to imagine such a God? And how far does God's friendship extend? Is it an accident that the one who initiates such covenant friendship in this story—Ruth—is an outsider? Not for the Israelites, for the Torah reminded them that God "loves the strangers," and that they were to "love the stranger, for you were strangers in the land of Egypt" (Dt 10:18-19). They *knew* that God placed the stranger at the center of the covenant. What might it mean today that God can be found in the stranger?

This story is about being at the crossroads of life . . . and about choices made at those significant times. It is also about "return," with its many meanings . . . return home, return to God, return to life from death. How do unforeseen circumstances and our responses to those circumstances form and shape our identity?

And, it is about that age-old mystery of suffering and loss and the human response to such emptiness. Naomi, for example, has been compared to a female Job (see Ruth 1:19-21 and Job 10:1-17). Sometimes, as is true for Naomi, loss and suffering can feel like humiliation. What does it take to return to life, wholeness, and fullness?

Finally, there are those who name Ruth and Naomi as heroic. Faced with developments that they recognize as contrary to God's plan, Ruth and Naomi refuse to be victimized. They look around, analyze the situation, conspire (or breathe air together), and come up with plans to make the best they can of the future. As it turns out, they manage to affect the history of an entire nation. We might ask ourselves, what does it mean to be heroic today?

In summary, Ruth's story cuts across time and space. We know her story well: friendship. Relationships that heal. The nature of God. Suffering. Loss and emptiness. A bountiful harvest. Choices made at crossroads. The place of the stranger/the outsider in our lives. Working with things as they are in order to imagine what is not yet. This story will leave none of us untouched . . . with its beauty, simplicity, persistence, challenge, and affirmation.

## SOME RESOURCES

Fewell, Danna Nolan, and David Miller Gunn. *Compromising Redemption: Relating Characters in the Book of Ruth*. Louisville, KY: Westminster John Knox Press, 1990.

Kates, Judith A. and Gail Twersky Reimer, editors. *Reading Ruth: Contemporary Women Reclaim a Sacred Story*. New York: Ballantine Books, 1994.

LaCocque, Andre. "Ruth." In his *The Feminine Unconventional: Four Subversive Figures in Israel's Tradition*, pp. 84-116. Minneapolis, MN: Fortress Press, 1990.

Laffey, Alice L. *An Introduction to the Old Testament: A Feminist Perspective*. Philadelphia, PA: Fortress Press, 1988.

Levine, Amy-Jill. "Ruth." *In Women's Bible Commentary, Expanded Edition*. Ed. Carol A. Newsom and Sharon H. Ringe. Louisville, KY: Westminster John Knox Press, 1998, pp. 84-90.

Trible, Phyllis, "A Human Comedy." In her God and the Rhetoric of Sexuality, pp. 166-199, Philadelphia, PA: Fortress Press, 1978.

Weems, Renita J. "Blessed Be the Tie That Binds." In her *Just a Sister Away*, pp. 23-36. San Diego, CA: LuraMedia, 1988.

## NOTES

1. This may be an early form of levirate marriage, described in Deuteronomy 25:5-10. In that passage, the custom is limited to the brother of the deceased. In any case, he serves as a *go'el* or "redeemer," "one with the right

to redeem," a close relative who takes responsibility for protecting the rights of the family in the absence of the head of the family (in this case, Elimelech).

2.   Edited by Judith A. Kates and Gail Twersky Reimer (New York: Ballantine Books, 1994).

3.   Sallie McFague, *Models of God* (Philadelphia, PA: Fortress Press, 1987).

# ten

HILDEGARD OF BINGEN

# Wisdom Gives Us Creative Abundant Life

*Hildegard's Feast Day is the day of her death, September 17. This service was first celebrated outdoors, overlooking the lush hills of western New York. It might seem odd at first to be celebrating Hildegard's greening life in the fall, but on second thought it really fits. For this service reflects Hildegard's rootedness in the greening power of God, in the promise of yet another spring. And it also reflects her prophetic and sure knowledge of the interconnectedness of all of life. After all, the southern half of the globe is experiencing spring at the same time that we celebrate the glories of autumn.*

*Music is essential to this service, since Hildegard composed music for the honor and glory of God. How else could the beauty and joy of God's praise be expressed? Selections are suggested, but the music chosen must be a source of joy for each particular community. All music suggested here is available through GIA Publications, Inc., Chicago, Illinois, except for "Loving Hands" by Cary Ratcliff, which is published through Kairos Music Publishers, P.O. Box 10165, Rochester, NY 14610. It might also be possible to purchase recordings of Hildegard's music, which would be best used before the service and during the Ritual of Re-Claiming the Spirit's Vision. Ideally, there will be musicians to lead the singing, and they will be visible to the entire gathered assembly.*

*The use of liturgical dance is also suggested. Dancers could lead in the musicians, reader, and leader during the gathering hymn and lead everyone out at the end. Dance could also be part of the musical reflection pieces.*

*The environment is simple. Whether out of doors or inside, it is important to have reminders of God's greening power in the entire worship space. Central to the worship space is a table large enough to comfortably hold a large glass bowl of water, a pitcher, and a green bough of some kind. If the service is celebrated in the evening, it is also appropriate to have a candle on the table, with several candles scattered throughout the worship space. A lectern would be placed nearby to hold the scripture.*

Ministers:   Hildegard, leader, reader, cantor, musicians, and liturgical dancers

Materials:   large table, large glass bowl of water, pitcher, green bough, lectern, scripture

## Introductory Rites

### GATHERING

*Everyone is welcomed to this celebration of abundant life, and people are invited to introduce themselves to those around them.*

### GATHERING HYMN                                      *Please stand*

"Canticle of the Sun," text and tune by Marty Haugen, GIA Publications, Inc., © 1980. *During this hymn, dancers carrying streamers lead a procession that includes singers, reader, and leader.*

### OPENING PRAYER

Leader:   O Holy Spirit,
fiery comforter Spirit,
life of the life of all creatures,
holy are you,
you that are balm for the mortally wounded.
Holy are you, you that cleanse deep hurt.

All:   Fire of love, breath of all holiness,
you are so delicious to our hearts.
You infuse our hearts deeply with the good smell of virtue.
You are the mighty way in which everything
that is in the heavens, on the earth,

and under the earth, is penetrated with connectedness,
is penetrated with relatedness.

Leader:     Through you clouds billow, breezes blow,
stones drip with trickling streams,
streams that are the source of earth's lush greening.

All:     Likewise,
you are the source of human understanding.
You bless with the breath of wisdom.
Thus all of our praise is yours.
You are the melody itself of praise,
the joy of life, the mighty honor, the hope
of those to whom you give the gifts of the light.

(Prayer by Hildegard of Bingen)

## Liturgy of the Word

● ● ● ● ● ● ● ● ● ● ● ● ● ● ● ● ● ● ● ● ● ● ● ● ● ● ● ● ● ● ● ● ● ● ● ● ● ● ● ● ● ● ● ● ● ● ● ●

PHILIPPIANS 2:1-11                         *Please be seated*
● ● ● ● ● ● ● ● ● ● ● ● ● ●

PSALM 34
● ● ● ● ● ● ● ●

"Taste and See," text and tune by James Moore, GIA Publications, Inc.,
© 1983.

JOHN 15:1-17
● ● ● ● ● ● ● ● ● ●

HOMILY *(Hildegard)*
● ● ● ● ● ● ● ● ● ● ● ●

Abundant life! Picture it! Clouds billowing, breezes blowing, stones dripping with trickling streams, earth's lush greening, the joy of life! What gives *you* abundant life?

Let me tell you the story of a friend. Now this happened just a few months ago, at the baptism of her grandson. She'd been invited to preach at the service, one of life's joys for her. It's important to tell you that her grandson was only two months old at the time. The minute she began speaking her grandson looked right at her. And continued to look at her, the entire time. Not only that, he started to smile at her . . . and continued to smile the whole time she was talking. After a couple of moments of this, she said her eyes filled with tears . . . at his attentiveness . . . but she also wanted to laugh. She didn't dare look at him for fear of totally losing her train of thought. She was convinced that he was just waiting for her to cover her eyes . . . then open them wide . . . and announce, "Peek a boo!" Now that's a story of abundant life!

What gives *you* abundant life? Here's some of what it is for me. Being creative. Writing music or poetry. Painting pictures. Preaching. Praising God, in the best way I know how. Sharing the beauty of my God-given visions. Urging the women in the monastery to nurture the many, varied green gifts that God has planted within them, that they might sprout and blossom and bloom, with joy for their Maker.

How did I learn about this greening power of God? Or *veriditas*, as I like to name it? First of all, by growing up in the beautiful Rhine Valley that I call home, with all its lush greenness and its fruitful vineyards. By paying attention to the God who dazzles in nature . . . and the visions that came to me from the time I was five years old. By paying attention to the living God who oozes life into the vine and the branches . . . into each and every one of us . . . and all creation besides.

What is Jesus saying to us in this juicy image of the vine and the branches? Just this, I believe. That God is abundant life and Jesus is greenness incarnate. That the Holy Spirit is greening power in motion, irrepressible love that can *never* be stopped from God's side. What does this kind of love look like? It does not know domination, one over another. Only mutual love, bringing out the best in one another. For the One to whom we bend our knee has washed our feet, commanding only this: "Love *one another* as I have loved you." Simple . . . but costly. For the greening power of Jesus came out of a tree that everyone thought was surely dead.

And I, myself, have known the cost. I buried a young nobleman on our monastery grounds, knowing that he had been reconciled to the church just before he died. But church officials regarded him as an excommunicated sinner and refused to honor my testimony in his behalf. They even placed the monastery under interdict, meaning that we couldn't celebrate the eucharist or sing the divine office. But I knew that I had done what was right, and protested mightily to the Archbishop of Mainz. Not long after that, just before my death, the interdict was finally removed from our monastery.

This kind of greening power can happen anywhere. Around the kitchen table. Or around one of your famous CEO boardroom tables. And—most certainly—it must always happen around Christ's table. For Jesus left us with the words of greening power, "Love one another as I have loved you."

## MUSICAL REFLECTION

"Loving Hands," music and text by Cary Ratcliff, Kairos Music Publishers, © 1991.

or

"Be Light for Our Eyes," text and tune by David Haas, GIA Publications, Inc., © 1985.

## INTERCESSIONS

Please respond, "O God, give us your greening power."

*What needs healing? Greening? Bringing to awareness? Life? Joy? In preparation, create prayers from the needs of the community; during the prayer itself, the presider will also invite prayers from the people.*

# Ritual of Re-Claiming the Spirit's Vision

## INVITATION AND PRAYER OF HILDEGARD         *Please stand*

Leader:     Who are the prophets?

All:        They are a royal people
            who penetrate mystery
            and see with the Spirit's eyes.
            In illuminated darkness they speak out.

Leader:     They are living, penetrating clarity.
            They are a blossom blooming only
            on the shoot that is rooted
            in the flood of light.

## BLESSING OF THE WATER

"Spirit Blowing Through Creation," text and tune by Marty Haugen, GIA Publications, Inc., © 1987.

*The presider invites everyone to extend an arm in blessing during the singing of the last verse and refrain.*

## INVITATION TO COME TO THE WATER

*As you return, please be seated*

*The presider invites each person forward to name a desire to "see," inspired by the Spirit of God. For example, "I seek healing . . . wisdom . . . understanding . . . illumination . . . something more specific" . . .*

*As the presider touches your eyes with water, she will listen to your desire and then respond, "_____, may the Spirit of God grant you your desire."*

## MUSIC DURING THE RITUAL

"Ubi Caritas" (text based on 1 Cor 13:2-8, "Where charity and love are found, God is there"), Taize Community, 1978; tune by Jacques Berthier, GIA Publications, Inc., © 1979, Les Presses de Taize.

or

"Veni Sancte Spiritus," text "Come Holy Spirit," with verses drawn from the Pentecost Sequence; Taize Community, 1978; tune by Jacques Berthier, GIA Publications, Inc., agent, © 1979, Les Presses de Taize.

or

*You might also use taped music by Hildegard of Bingen.*

# Closing Rites

## PRAYER OF COMING TOGETHER AS ONE

*Please stand and join hands in a circle*

Leader:    In Nature, God established humankind in power.
           We are dressed in the scaffold of creation:

All:    In seeing—to recognize all the world,
        in hearing—to understand,
        in smelling—to discern,
        in tasting—to nurture,
        in touching—to govern.

Leader: In this way humankind comes to know God,
        for God is the author of all creation.

(Prayer by Hildegard of Bingen)

## PRAYER OF SENDING

Leader: Be not lax in celebrating;
        be not lazy in the festive service of God.
        Be ablaze with enthusiasm.
        Let us be an alive,
        burning offering
        before the altar of God!
        (Hildegard of Bingen)

All:    Now and forevermore! Amen! Alleluia!

## CLOSING HYMN

"You Are the Voice," text and tune by David Haas, GIA Publications, Inc., © 1983, 1987.

# Hildegard of Bingen

She was forty-two years old when she felt the certain and persistent call of God. Oh, she had responded to God before. And she had grown in her understanding of God and her work in this world. Yet, she was uncertain. Did God really mean for her, a mere woman with no formal education, to write down everything she saw and understood? There was still doubt, passivity, uncertainty that God could possibly mean her.

Does this sound familiar? Is it a contemporary woman's struggle to come to terms with God's purposes? A church's struggle to believe that woman has anything of value to say? Yes. And more. This is an account of a remarkably gifted woman rooted in and watered by her lush twelfth-century Rhineland. For Hildegard was a Renaissance woman at least three centuries before the flowering of the Renaissance in the Italian city-states: a poet, artist, musician, healer drawn to the science of the human body, Benedictine abbess, prophet who confronted church and secular leaders alike, preacher, and mystic of timeless Wisdom.

> God says:
> In the shaking out of my mantle
> you are drenched,
> watered,
> with thousands upon thousands
> of drops
> of precious dew.
> Thus is humanity gifted.[1]

## THE LANDSCAPE
## OF THIS DIVINELY WATERED, GIFTED WOMAN

Imagine this. As a child, you cast your eye over a lush green valley. It is the valley of the Nahe River, which meanders below, emptying into the Rhine at nearby Bingen. As an adult, the landscape beyond your monastery is alive with greenness, as far as the eye can see. Vineyards producing juicy grapes. Fir trees. Lush grass. This is the world of Hildegard. Is it any wonder that she creates the word "*veriditas*," a single word to capture the greening power of God? *Veriditas* is the power of springtime, of creation, the life force in humans and, indeed, the entire earth. For her, the Holy Spirit is greening power in motion and Jesus is greenness incarnate. And "the earth sweats germinating power from its very pores."[2]

Now further imagine a time when most of the people work the land, tied to the estate of a noble. The church has enormous influence over everyone's daily life, through Benedictine monasteries formed as far back as the sixth century—the old centers of learning—and newer orders with a reform-minded spirit (e.g., the Carthusians are formed in 1084 and the Cistercians in 1098). And the popes, especially since the time of Gregory VII (d. 1085), claim enormous power over all Christians. There is stability, and yet change is in the air. Emperors and kings, vying for more control, challenge even the pope, naming several antipopes during the twelfth century. One of these is Holy Roman Emperor Frederick Barbarossa, one of several rulers with whom Hildegard corresponds. Gothic cathedrals, pointing the human spirit heavenward—magnificent structures like the one at Chartres—are being built. New centers of learning appear. The Cathedral School of Paris will soon join with others to become the University of Paris. The spread of Islam westward since the seventh century and the calling of the First Crusade in 1095 will wreak havoc and hatred, but will also further trade and the growth of towns. These are the times of Hildegard.

## THE EARLY YEARS

Hildegard's life spanned most of the twelfth century (1098-1179) and was spent in her native Rhineland, except for preaching tours late in her life. She was the tenth and last child of Hildebert (a knight attached to the Castle of Bickelheim) and Mechtild von Bermersheim. They dedicated her to God as an infant, possibly as a tithe, not an unusual practice at the time. She was "different," even as a youngster, admitting that her visions of God started at age five. When she was eight, she was placed under the tutelage of Jutta of Sponheim, a holy anchoress attached to the Benedictine monastery of Mount St. Disibode, named after a seventh-century Celtic monk who had settled in that region. From early on she was trained in the Benedictine way of biblical prayer and history, work, music, and spinning. At age eighteen she became a Benedictine and matured under the tutelage of her mentor and dear friend, Jutta. When Jutta died in 1136, Hildegard was chosen as her successor to lead the dozen women of her community.

## THE VISIONARY, IN HER OWN WORDS

Four years later she was to experience her awakening, the God of her visions calling her forth. Listen to her, as she describes her struggles around that life-changing event. "Ever since I was a girl—certainly from the time I was five years old right up to the present—in a wonderful way I had felt in myself (even as I do now) the strength and mystery of these secret and marvelous visions."[3] But I told no one, except a very few religious people I could trust. "I suppressed it beneath strict silence,"[4] for I came to know that other people didn't see what I saw. What were these visions like, you might want to know? "The visions which I saw I did not perceive in dreams nor when asleep nor in a delirium nor with the eyes or ears of the body. I received them when I was awake and looking around with a clear mind, with the inner eyes and ears, in open places according to the will of God. But how this could be,"[5] I do not know. And even I began to doubt. Who was I, anyway? Just a woman, and unlettered, at that. So, "I refused to write them until I fell upon my sickbed";[6] I silenced myself and became very ill.

And then, one day, it happened, my very own Pentecost. "In the year 1141 of the incarnation of Jesus Christ the Son of God, when I was forty-two years and seven months of age, a fiery light, flashing intensely, came from the open vault of heaven and poured through my whole brain. Like a flame that is hot without burning it kindled all my heart and all my breast, just as the sun warms anything on which its rays fall. And suddenly I could understand what such books as the Psalter, the Gospel, and the other Catholic volumes both of the Old and New Testament actually set forth. . . . "[7] Then I heard the voice of the living light. It was this voice who said to me—twice—"Cry out and write, therefore, the things you see and hear."[8] For I have chosen you, with all your insecurities, to write in your own way, out of your own heart. So, with the encouragement of the holy Bernard of Clairvaux and the archbishop of Mainz, I began to believe in myself. And, with the help of my faithful scribe Volmer and my dear friend, the nun Richardis of Stade, I set my hand to the writing. "And, raising myself from illness by the strength I received, I brought this work to a close—though just barely—in ten years."[9] I called it "Scito vias Domini" ("Know the Ways of the Lord"), but people usually referred to it as "Scivias."

And, as I often tell people, these visions continue. For "God works where he wills, for the glory of God's name and not for that of mortals. Indeed, I have always trembled with fear, since I am not confident of any ability in myself; but I hold out my hands to God so that I might be supported by him, like a feather . . . which flies on the wind."[10] So, to all of you who "seek these words . . . and desire to hear these things in faith, pray for me, that I may continue in the service of God."[11]

## ABBESS

Despite her inner conflicts, Hildegard was a strong abbess, acting out of her holiness and what she perceived to be in the best interests of the community. By 1148, Hildegard had attracted enough women to Mount St. Disibode that they outgrew their quarters. So Hildegard left with eighteen other women to form a new abbey for women at nearby Rupertsberg, but not without a struggle from the abbot and monks of Disibodenberg. They knew that Hildegard attracted people and money. But her persistence and strength prevailed, marking the blossoming of Hildegard's creativity, in the form of music, poetry, and drama at Rupertsberg. The new community grew to fifty sisters, and in 1156 she formed yet a third monastery across the river from Bingen at Eibingen. Truly, she lived her own words,

Be not lax
in celebrating,
be not lazy
in the festive service of God.
Be ablaze with enthusiasm.
Let us be an alive,
burning offering
before the altar of God![12]

## PROPHET

• • • • • • •

And Hildegard was a prophet, a spokeswoman for God, whose vibrant life included preaching to bishops and laity alike, and living out a passion surrounding an interdict shortly before her death. Although she found it difficult, she felt compelled to confront all leaders who did not live up to their responsibilities. Indeed, Bernard of Clairvaux—the well known holy abbot of the Cistercian motherhouse—was one of the few to go unchallenged by Hildegard. Early on, she praised King Frederick Barbarossa for his good name, while warning him of people everywhere who "put out the light of justice."[13] Urging him to live out his office rightly, she concluded, "May your times not be dry."[14] For Hildegard, dryness was the greatest sin, cutting oneself off from the moistness of God. Indeed, she did not hesitate to name the dryness she saw in him later, convicting Barbarossa of being a "madman" when he dared to appoint an antipope.

But her harshest words were reserved for the prelates of Mainz, who placed her monastery under interdict. This meant that there would be no eucharist or singing of the divine office. Hildegard had allowed the burial of a young nobleman on her grounds; the prelates knew he had been excommunicated, but Hildegard knew further that he had celebrated penance and been anointed before his death. Assured by God of the rightness of her cause, she bluntly warned them that the devil works best by removing the beauty of music. She concludes that "the harshest judgment will be pronounced [by God] on prelates who fail, in the words of the apostle, to carry out their office with caution [see Romans 12:8].[15] Finally, a letter from her to Archbishop Christian of Mainz resulted in the removal of the interdict only a few short months before her death on September 17.

It is said that she is a mystic of creation-centered spirituality. True, she is in love with all God's creation. But what a love affair she had with God! The God who is green. Moist. Juicy. Penetrating, linking all people and all of creation. Let her words speak:

> Who is the Trinity?
> You are music.
> You are life.
> Source of everything,
> Creator of everything,
> angelic hosts sing your praise.
> Wonderfully radiant,
> deep,
> mysterious.
> You are alive in everything,
> and yet you are unknown to us.[16]

For her, creation "is allowed in intimate love, to speak to the Creator as if to a lover."[17] But, what awesome wonder that only people can sing praise to God—not unlike the angels—and do good works! People alone can be co-creators, "useful" (a favorite word) in doing God's good works of justice and compassion. For the God who so generously gives also expects human sweat in the use of these gifts. And abundant fruitfulness is the promised result.

As Hildegard so often remarked, she did not fully understand the visions or the words that were given to her. Hers are the prophetic words of interdependence. Today, in a world that has known the atomic bomb and the Holocaust, the struggles against racism, sexism, and heterosexism, her words ring true. We understand the call, the deep need, to honor all creation. We understand the cost of *not* respecting life. Her words remain compelling in a world where the violence of battering (emotionally, spiritually, physically, economically) or not caring threatens our very existence. Listen to her challenge us: "The ultimate not-caring or carelessness occurs when we become cold and hardened to injustice."[18]

Ultimately, Hildegard—that moist, greening, fruitful, poetic woman who is a mystic—challenges us by her very person to be prophets of joy. "Who are the prophets? They are a royal people, who penetrate mystery and see with the spirit's eyes. In illuminating darkness they speak out.

They are living, penetrating clarity. They are a blossom blooming only on the shoot that is rooted in the flood of light."[19]

## SOME RESOURCES
• • • • • • • • • • • • • • •

Bowie, Fiona and Oliver Davies, editors. *Hildegard of Bingen: Mystical Writings.* New York: Crossroad, 1990.

Durka, Gloria. *Praying with Hildegard of Bingen.* Winona, MN: Saint Mary's Press, 1991.

Fox, Matthew. *Illuminations of Hildegard of Bingen: Text by Hildegard of Bingen with Commentary by Matthew Fox, O.P.* Santa Fe, NM: Bear & Company, 1985.

_____, editor. *Hildegard of Bingen's Book of Divine Works, with Letters and Songs.* Santa Fe, NM: Bear & Company, 1987.

Hart, Mother Columba and Jane Bishop, translators. *Scivias.* Mahwah, NJ: Paulist Press, 1990.

Uhlein, Gabriele. *Meditations with Hildegard of Bingen.* Santa Fe, NM: Bear & Company, 1983.

## NOTES
• • • • •

1. Gabriele Uhlein, *Meditations with Hildegard of Bingen* (Santa Fe, NM: Bear & Company, 1983), p. 109; hereafter referred to as Uhlein.

2. Matthew Fox, *Illuminations of Hildegard of Bingen: Text by Hildegard of Bingen with Commentary by Matthew Fox, O.P.* (Santa Fe, NM: Bear & Co., 1985), p. 32; hereafter referred to as *Illuminations.*

3. Hildegard of Bingen, *Mystical Writings*, edited and introduced by Fiona Bowie and Oliver Davies (New York: Crossroad, 1990), p. 68; hereafter referred to as Bowie and Davies.

4. Ibid., p. 68.

5. Ibid., p. 68.

6. Ibid., p. 70.

7. Ibid., p. 68.

8. Hildegard of Bingen, *Scivias*, translated by Mother Columba Hart and Jane Bishop (Mahwah, NJ: Paulist Press, 1990), pp. 60-61.

9. Ibid., p. 61.

10. Bowie and Davies, p. 145.

11.  Ibid., p. 147.

12.  Uhlein, p. 128.

13.  Matthew Fox, editor, *Hildegard of Bingen Book of Divine Works, with Letters and Songs* (Santa Fe, NM: Bear & Company, 1987), p. 289.

14.  Ibid., p. 290.

15.  Ibid., p. 359.

16.  Uhlein, p. 28.

17.  Ibid., p. 57.

18.  *Illuminations*, p. 64.

19.  Uhlein, p. 126.

# eleven

# JULIAN OF NORWICH

# We Find Joy in All Things

........................................................................

*Julian of Norwich was a fourteenth-century English anchoress, a woman attached to St. Julian's Church. In effect, she had taken a vow to become the heart of God's compassion for a suffering humanity. The companion paper gives helpful information to planners of the liturgy.*

*It is important to have flowers and plants in the gathering space and throughout the worship space. Greeters will include Julian as Worship Leader, who will hand out a program, pencil, and a heart-shaped paper to each participant.*

*The focus of the worship space will be a table, covered with a white cloth. It will be large enough to comfortably hold a vase of flowers, a small clear dish of hazelnuts,[1] and a large paper heart, similar to but larger than the one given to each participant. A large basket decorated with ribbon is on the floor in front of the table. To one side of the table is the lectern, from which the psalms and other readings are proclaimed.*

Ministers:   *Julian, two voices, cantor, and musicians*

Materials:   *table covered with a white cloth, vase of flowers, basket, clear bowl of hazelnuts (or acorns), additional flowers and plants, a large paper heart and smaller paper hearts, pencils*

---

# Introductory Rites

*Julian introduces herself and other leaders and invites others to do the same with one another.*

## CALL TO WORSHIP
*Please stand*

Julian:    O God + of every breath, our beginning and our end,
O God of burning passion and most tender compassion,
unbind our sin and our tongues this day,
that we may joyfully praise your name.

All:    For "our substance is in" you[2]
loving Father of "almighty truth,"
loving Mother of "deep wisdom."[3]
Heal our broken hearts and restore us,
make us one with you, with each other
and with your entire creation.

Julian:    For you have assured us:
"I may make things well,
and I can make all things well,
and I shall make all things well,
and I will make all things well;
and you will see for yourself
that every kind of thing will be well."[4]

## OPENING HYMN

"Morning Hymn," text by David Haas, tune adapted by David Haas from Summit Hill, GIA Publications, Inc., © 1987.

# Liturgy of the Word

## PSALM 63

"In the Shadow of Your Wings," text by David Haas (based on Psalm 63), tune by David Haas, GIA Publications, Inc., © 1986.

*Silence*

## PSALM 16
· · · · · · ·

"Center of My Life," text is Psalm 16, verses trans. GIA Publications, Inc., © 1963, 1993 by The Grail, refrain and tune by Paul Inwood, OCP Publications, © 1985. *Some might want to change the words that begin the refrain from "O Lord" to "O God."*

*Silence*

## A READING FROM PAUL'S LETTER TO THE PHILIPPIANS AND JULIAN OF NORWICH[5]
· · · · · · · · · · · · · · · · · · · · · ·

*Voice 1:*

Rejoice in the Lord always; again I will say, rejoice. Let your gentleness be known to everyone. The Lord is near (Phil 4:4-5).

*Voice 2:*

"And with this our good Lord said most joyfully: See how I love you, as if he had said, my darling, behold and see . . . your God, who is your Creator and your endless joy; see your own brother, your savior; my child, behold and see what delight and bliss I have in your salvation, and for my love rejoice with me.

"And for my greater understanding, these blessed words were said: See how I love you, as if he had said, behold and see that I loved you so much, before I died for you, that I wanted to die for you. And now I have died for you, and willingly suffered what I could. And now all my bitter pain and my hard labor is turned into everlasting joy and bliss for me and for you. How could it now be that you would pray to me for anything pleasing to me which I would not very gladly grant to you? For my delight is in your holiness and in your endless joy and bliss in me."

*Voice 1:*

Do not worry about anything, but in everything by prayer and supplication with thanksgiving let your requests be made known to God. And the peace of God, which surpasses all understanding, will guard your hearts and your minds in Christ Jesus (Phil 4:6-7).

## REFLECTION *(Julian)*

Life is hard. I have seen it . . . and wrestled with it. And I hear about it all the time from the people who come to me. Yes, I know about the violent, sudden death of loved ones in the plague . . . of fathers and sons killed in the war with France . . . of all the struggles of daily living. But I have seen more, so very much more. I have seen that God "is to us everything which is good and comforting for our help."[6] I have seen "a revelation of love which Jesus Christ, our endless bliss, made in sixteen showings."[7] And I *must* tell you about this, for these visions are not just for me but for everyone.

It all began like this. I was always drawn to God in prayer, as long as I can remember. And I began to see how much Christ loved us. It was then that I *longed* to see his Passion with my own eyes, just like his first friends. This was granted to me when I was thirty-and-a-half years old. The pain and the grief is beyond description. But, just as I thought I would see Jesus die . . . and nearly die myself . . . his whole face beamed with joy for all he had done for each of us.

Jesus tenderly asked, "Are you well satisfied that I suffered for you?"[8] "Oh, *yes!*" The words tumbled out and he went on. "If you are satisfied, I am satisfied. It is a joy, a bliss, an endless delight to me that ever I suffered my Passion for you; and if I could suffer more, I should suffer more."[9] And I saw "that the love in him which he has for our souls was so strong that he willingly chose suffering with a great desire, and suffered it meekly with a great joy."[10]

## MUSICAL RESPONSE

"Blest Are Those Who Love You," refrain 1 only, sung twice. Text by Marty Haugen (based on Psalm 128), tune by Marty Haugen, GIA Publications, Inc., © 1987.

But I was troubled. I could see that God, in divine goodness, never blames or becomes angry. "And then I saw that only pain blames and punishes, and our courteous Lord comforts . . . and always . . . is kindly disposed to the soul, loving and longing to bring us to . . . bliss."[11] Indeed, I believed God's assurance that "I will make all things well."[12] But *why* did sin exist? So I dared to ask, "Ah, good Lord, how could all things be well, because of the great harm which has come through sin to your creatures?"[13] For I knew all too well about "my" own "weakness, wretchedness and blindness."[14] So God responded to my questions with a parable, of a lord and his servant.

> The lord sits in state, in rest and in peace. The servant stands before his lord, respectfully, ready to do his lord's will. The lord looks on his servant very lovingly and sweetly and mildly. He sends him to a certain place to do his will. Not only does the servant go, but he dashes off and runs at great speed, loving to do his lord's will. And soon he falls into a dell and is greatly injured; and then he groans and moans and tosses about and writhes, but he cannot rise or help himself in any way. And of all this, the greatest hurt which I saw him in was lack of consolation, for he could not turn his face to look on his loving lord, who was very close to him, in whom is all consolation; but like [someone] who was for the time extremely feeble and foolish, he paid heed to his feelings and his continuing distress, in which he suffered seven great pains." And these were "bruising," "clumsiness," "weakness," blindness and perplexity, inability to get up, isolation, and the discomfort of a "narrow" and "distressful" place.[15]

I did not understand. So God said, "See my beloved servant, what harm and injuries he has had and accepted in my service for my love, yes, and for his good will. Is it not reasonable that I should reward him for his fright and his fear, his hurt and his injuries? And furthermore, is it not proper for me to give him a gift, better for him and more honorable than his own health could have been? Otherwise, it seems to me that I should be ungracious."[16] In some way, as I saw, mature love that is tested in the fire of service becomes a badge of honor, shining with love for its Maker, more pleasing to God than naïve innocence. And God thanks us greatly and endlessly for our service.[17]

*Silence*

## MUSICAL RESPONSE

"Blest Are Those Who Love You," refrain 1 only, sung twice. Text by Marty Haugen (based on Psalm 128), tune by Marty Haugen, GIA Publications, Inc., © 1987.

But I *still* did not understand. So God told me to pay close attention to all that was happening. I noticed that the lord was sitting in the wilderness. And, after nearly twenty years, it was revealed to me that God is the lord, who had "made" human souls "to be his own . . . dwelling place."[18] After the onslaught of sin, God waited in the wilderness until the "beloved Son" had restored the human soul to "its noble place of beauty by his hard labor."[19] Then I noticed that God's regard for the servant "could melt our hearts for love and break them in two for joy."[20] What a mixture of compassion and pity, joy and bliss! "The compassion and the pity of" God "were for Adam, who is his most beloved creature. The joy and the bliss were for the falling of his dearly beloved Son, who is equal with the Father."[21]

The servant is Adam—each of us—who turns away from God, becomes blind, isolated and weak, all the while longing to serve God. And the servant is Jesus, "our true Mother Jesus,"[22] who labored long and hard on the cross, to restore us to our real home in God. This was "the beginning of an ABC, whereby I may have some understanding" of God's meaning.[23] For I see that God chooses to reveal some of the divine mystery to us now; the rest will only come in the fullness of time.

But this much I already know. For it was God who said it. "Everything" . . . even this little hazelnut (*Julian holds up a hazelnut*) . . . "has being through the love of God. It lasts and always will, because God loves it. . . ."[24] But we—every one of us—are "the noblest thing" of all, "knitted to" God from the beginning.[25] And then God assured me. "You will not be overcome"[26] . . . for "I protect you very safely."[27] And these words were "said with more love and assurance of protection for my soul than I can or may tell."[28]

And, finally, I know this. This vision is not complete, for we continue to live it.[29] Jesus continues to thirst for us. That we might turn to him, again and again, accepting "our sufferings as lightly as we are able."[30] For "our true Mother Jesus . . . alone bears us for joy and for endless life."[31] Why? "For love."[32] In love. And through love.

## GOSPEL CANTICLE
. . . . . . . . . . . . . .

"Blest Are They," text by David Haas (based on Matthew 5:3-12), tune by David Haas, GIA Publications, Inc., © 1985.

# Ritual of Healing

There is a fracture at our very core. We hurt ourselves and others. We harm the world around us. Truly, we are heartbroken. We know how this feels. We may get depressed. Even despairing. Or ashamed. And angry with ourselves for all our failures. Which is why joy is so hard to come by. For joy is *not* a superficial happiness. It is *not* a denial that there is anything wrong. On the contrary, it is a realistic probing of our very depths. It requires a willingness to take a good long look at what's right and what's wrong, both within and without. It requires finding God at our very core. The God "who created everything for love . . ." who is "everything which is good. . . ."[33] The God who "wishes to be known . . ." who wants us to "come . . . openly and familiarly."[34] The God who "is our clothing, who wraps and enfolds us for love, embraces and shelters us, surrounds us for . . . love," and will "never desert us."[35] It requires healing at our core by the Christ whose passion for us burned brightly on the cross, whose love named each of us priceless and worth the horrendous cost. It requires healing by this God, in Christ, who alone is the source of our identity and our joy.

I invite you to take a moment now. Consider that sacred space within, where God dwells. Consider bringing the world of your deepest need and your deepest desire to that space. Consider any brokenness of heart. Consider any desire for healing and joy. And, when you are ready, come forward to say, "God of all goodness. I need . . . and want your healing touch. Give me your joy, I pray." Then place your heart in this basket as a sign of your desire for and commitment to healing and joy.

## MUSIC DURING THE RITUAL

"Healer of Our Every Ill," text and tune by Marty Haugen, GIA Publications, Inc., © 1987.

or

"Ubi Caritas" (text based on 1 Corinthians 13:2-8, Where charity and love are found, God is there), Taize Community, 1978; tune by Jacques Berthier, Les Presses de Taize, GIA Publications, Inc., © 1979.

## INTERCESSIONS

• • • • • • • • • • • • •

*Julian places the basket on the table. All the unspoken intentions contained in these hearts will be included in the prayer.*

Julian:    We can never doubt the "high, surpassing, immeasurable love" which God has for us; "therefore we may, with reverence, ask from our lover all that we will. . . . For God's good will is to have us, and we can never stop willing or loving until we possess [God] in the fullness of joy."[36] Therefore, we have the courage and trust to pray. . . .

Sung refrain (*at the beginning and end and after every third petition*), "Memorial Acclamation 4: Good and gracious God, hear and remember us," "Eucharistic Prayer II," Marty Haugen, GIA Publications, Inc., © 1990.

## THE LORD'S PRAYER

• • • • • • • • • • • • • • • • • •

Julian:    Let us pray as Jesus taught us, remembering that God is both Father and Mother to us. For truly I saw that "our true Mother Jesus" labored on the Cross for us . . . and feeds "us with himself . . . and with all the sweet sacraments he sustains us most mercifully and graciously. . . ."[37] Therefore, we begin by saying Our Father/Mother. . . .

# Closing Rites

• • • • • • • • • • • • • • • • • • • • • • • • • • • • • • • • • • • • • • •

## BLESSING

• • • • • • • •

Julian:    God, the Trinity, "filled my heart full of the greatest joy.
For the Trinity is God, God is the Trinity.
The Trinity is our maker, the Trinity is our protector,
the Trinity is our everlasting lover,
the Trinity is our endless joy and our bliss,
by our Lord Jesus Christ and in our Lord Jesus Christ."[38]

All:      Blessed be our God!

Julian:    Go forth, + then, in the sign of God's love and joy
to serve our living God, each other, and all God's creation.

All:      Amen! Alleluia! Let it be!

## CLOSING HYMN
● ● ● ● ● ● ● ● ● ● ● ● ●

"Joyful, Joyful, We Adore You," text by Henry van Kyke, © Charles Scribner's Sons; tune is "Ode to Joy" by Ludwig van Beethoven.

## NOTES
● ● ● ● ●

1. God showed Julian a hazelnut. She says, "I was amazed that it could last, for I thought that because of its littleness it would suddenly have fallen into nothing. And I was answered in my understanding: It lasts and always will, because God loves it; and thus everything has being through the love of God." This is found in Julian, LT 5, p. 183.

2. Julian, LT 55, p. 287.

3. Julian, LT 54, p. 285.

4. Julian, LT 31, p. 229.

5. See Philippians 4:4-7 and Julian, LT 24, p. 221.

6. Julian, LT 5, p. 183.

7. Julian, LT 1, p. 175.

8. Julian, LT 22, p. 216.

9. Ibid.

10. Julian, LT 20, p. 214.

11. Julian, LT 51, p. 271.

12. Julian, LT 31, p. 229.

13. Julian, LT 29, p. 227.

14. Julian, LT 66, p. 310.

15. Julian, LT 51, pp. 267-68.

16. Julian, LT 51, pp. 268-69.

17. Julian, LT 14, p. 203 and LT 84, p. 340.

18. Julian, LT 51, p. 272.

19. Ibid.

20. Julian, LT 51, p. 271.

21. Ibid.

22. Julian, LT 63, p. 298.

23. Julian, LT 51, p. 276.

24. Julian, LT 5, p. 183.

25. Julian, LT 53, p. 284.

26. Julian, LT 68, p. 315.

27. Julian, LT 37, p. 241.

28. Ibid.

29. Julian, LT 86, p. 342.

30. Julian, LT 64, pp. 307-308.

31. Julian, LT 60, p. 298.

32. Julian, LT 86, p. 342.

33. These quotes are from Julian, LT 8, p. 190.

34. These quotes are from Julian, LT 5, p. 184.

35. Julian, LT 5, p. 183.

36. Julian, LT 6, p. 186. I have written God in brackets to make the language inclusive.

37. Julian, LT 63, p. 298.

38. Julian, LT 4, p. 181.

## Julian of Norwich

Julian is not her real name. But that is how we know her, for she was attached as an anchoress in the fourteenth century to St. Julian's Church in Norwich, England. Julian is a most remarkable woman of mature faith. Realistic. And courageous, daring to pray for an experience of Christ's Passion. Daring to ponder and to question the deepest questions of human existence: the seeming paradox of God's love and human sin and suffering. In the next few pages, this woman will be explored and appreciated through the lenses of her times, her ministry as an anchoress, her visions, and her theology.

The times were difficult. It was the fourteenth century, a time of warfare. Trouble brewed with Scotland and France; and when a papal call for a Crusade crumbled, military energies were diverted into a prolonged conflict between England and France. This would become known as the Hundred Years War. It was also the time of the Black Death. "People died, horribly, suddenly and in great numbers. It was so contagious that," according to one contemporary witness, "anyone who touched the sick or the dead immediately caught the disease and died . . . , so that priests who ministered to the dying were flung into the same grave with their penitents."[1] Terror spread with the disease, which came in unpredictable cycles. The Black Death began in Dorset, England, in 1348, and spread to Norwich in January of the following year, when Julian was just a girl of seven. Two more severe outbreaks ravaged the countryside in 1361 and 1369. Probably a third of this city's population and half its clergy perished in the plague. Famine reared its ugly head, as well, and was especially severe in the last year of the plague.

This was the final straw for peasants already taxed to the breaking point; a peasants' revolt began in the south, led by Wat Tyler, and spread like wildfire throughout England. There was looting. Even monasteries were not exempt from the plunder. Government and some church officials, as well, harshly retaliated. Bishop Henry Despenser of Norwich, for example, was well known for his arrogance, ostentatious display of wealth, and his ruthless quelling of the riots.

The official church of the fourteenth century was in a sad state. During Julian's entire lifetime (from December 1342 until ca. 1416), the papacy was in a shambles. It was the time of the "Babylonian Captivity," when popes lived in Avignon, under the control of the French king. When Pope Gregory XI finally returned to Rome in 1377, his successor, Urban VI, was challenged by a second so-called pope, Clement VII. This Great Schism lasted another forty years, until the 1417 election of Pope Martin V. In England, the beginning of a Crusade, called by Urban VI and led by Bishop Despenser, disintegrated shamefully into looting of French territory and abuse of indulgences. On the level of popular piety, eucharistic devotion often deteriorated into the practice of host gazing, which some believed would prevent aging.

Such practices cried out for reform. And in fourteenth-century England John Wycliffe, an influential Oxford scholar, was among the prominent voices raised for change. He and his followers, known as Lollards, opposed clericalism and other abuses that kept people from experiencing the gospel through the church. And, they were responsible for the first English translation of the entire Bible, published in 1390. But they were also roundly condemned as heretics by the official church; some, in fact, were burned to death by the turn of the fifteenth century. It is worthwhile noting that Julian undoubtedly was aware of all this, for her anchorhold was just barely out of sight of the place of execution. It is also worth noting that Julian wrote in English, herself, precisely to make her work accessible to people. For while she professed allegiance to the church, whose essence is Christ, she could not condone any abusive behavior within the church. Indeed, she saw that sin "has no kind of substance, no share in being, nor can it be recognized except by the pain caused by it."[2]

Norwich in the fourteenth century was a thriving port city in southeastern England, just enough inland on the Wensum River to escape the threats of piracy further south in the English Channel. Trade in wool and other fabric thrived with Flanders to the east; and Norwich became a gateway to London, to its southwest, and other significant cities. Norwich was also home to all the major religious orders of its time, including an informal social action-oriented sisterhood known as the Beguines.[3] But the Benedictines were foremost among the orders there; its cathedral priory was a recognized center of learning in Julian's time. It is not clear whether or not she might have attended the boarding school at Carrow Abbey, a well-known Benedictine "nunnery," just outside the city walls. If she did, her education would have been somewhat limited, compared to what was available to the men of her day. A formal education for men included Latin and the classics; in the nunneries, even among the Benedictines, the majority of women knew no Latin. "The whole trend of medieval thought was against learned women. . . . While the monks composed chronicles, the nuns embroidered copes. . . ."[4] But Julian was a very bright woman, who somehow immersed herself in scripture and the tradition; her prayerful pondering of both, as well as her visions, produced a work of remarkable insight and skill.

## JULIAN AS ANCHORESS

"Do you not know that all of us who have been baptized into Christ Jesus were baptized into his death? Therefore we have been buried with him by baptism into death, so that, just as Christ was raised from the dead by the glory of the Father, so we too might walk in newness of life.

For if we have been united with him in a death like his, we will certainly be united with him in a resurrection like his."[5]

An anchorite (male) or anchoress (female) is named from the Greek word meaning "to retire."[6] The anchoress, like Julian, "retired" from all the normal activity of the world in order to create a prayerful, compassionate, womb-like space, where the cares of the world could be brought before God for nurturing. Rooted in the spirituality of the fourth-century desert fathers and mothers, the anchoress developed her "solitude in towns and villages: being in the world but not of it. . . . "[7] When she entered the anchorhold, she celebrated her death to the world in the Rite of Enclosure. "In the Sarum usage, to which others are similar, a requiem Mass was sung at the church. Then there was a solemn procession to the anchorhold," which was blessed. "The anchoress was then given extreme unction, after which the bishop scattered dust on the anchoress and the anchorhold, which from henceforward was to be considered her grave. The bishop then left the anchoress inside, and bolted the door on the outside, after which the procession returned to the church."[8] Now her primary responsibility would be prayer, but she would also actively and compassionately listen to all who came to her. And prayer was to become her way of being involved in the world; prayer would become the avenue for God's compassion to flow to all who would seek her out.

It took a mature person to honor this kind of life. It's true: she was "cared for" by the church. She lived in a small set of rooms, with a window onto the church for Mass in one, and a small window onto the outside world in another, for those who would seek her guidance. She had a servant, as well, who would see to her food and other daily needs. But, there were numerous temptations. The life of having only minimal contact with a servant and confessor, or with those who would seek guidance from her, could lead to feelings of isolation, boredom, loneliness, and even desolation. Then there might be a temptation to gossip, with one's servant or visitor. Or to sexual misconduct. Or even a temptation to almsgiving, a good thing, which could become a distraction from her main responsibility. The author of the *Ancrene Riwle*, an early thirteenth-century rule of life for anchoresses, also cautioned against the temptation to become a schoolmistress, for the same reason.[9] On a lighter note, the same author considers it a bad idea for an anchoress to keep cows. "Christ knoweth, it is an odious thing when people in the town complain of anchoresses' cattle."[10] On the positive side, she was encouraged to stay in good health and maintain a balance in her life, with no extremes of asceticism. "The anchoress, after all, was not to be a seven day wonder of ascetical heroics, but a life-long witness of dedication to prayer and holiness."[11] Again, the author of the *Ancrene Riwle* says it all: "They who love most shall be most blessed, not they who lead the most austere life, for love outweigheth this."[12] But even love might bring a temptation to "fix" what was wrong. From this she must abstain. Rather, she must become "the place where the love of God patiently takes to itself the pain of the world, and thereby brings lasting healing."[13] This was a very large order, and Julian of Norwich faced that challenge with all the grace that grew in her and flowed from her.

## JULIAN THE VISIONARY

Julian had passionately prayed for a "recollection of the Passion," so that she "might have more knowledge of our saviour's bodily pains, and of the compassion of our Lady and of all his true lovers . . . for" she "would have been one of them and have suffered with them."[14] She had also prayed for a "bodily sickness," severe and full of pain, so as "to be purged by God's mercy, and afterwards live more to [God's] glory."[15] Finally, she prayed for three wounds: "the wound of true contrition, the wound of loving compassion and the wound of longing with my will for God," asking "urgently for this third without any condition."[16] These prayers were granted in May 1373. She became deathly ill for three days and three nights. She received the last rites, and just as it seemed she might die, the curate set a crucifix in front of her, suggesting that she focus on it. She did. And she was graced with "a revelation of love which Jesus Christ, our endless bliss, made in sixteen showings."[17] She experienced the many horrors of Jesus' Passion and death: "well-being, [with its] true certainty of endless joy" and woe; "the heaviness and weariness of our mortal life"; the delight of the Trinity in Jesus' loving labor for each of us on the cross; "an exalted spiritual showing" of Mary, the mother of Jesus; the mystery that "all will be well" despite human sin; the certain knowledge that God totally treasures all humanity and that "our Lord God is the foundation of our beseeching"; the truth that "suddenly we shall be taken from all our pain" and filled with "joy and bliss in heaven"; and the ultimate truth "that the blessed Trinity our Creator dwells eternally in our soul in Christ Jesus our saviour."[18] She immediately committed these visions to paper, knowing that they were for everyone.[19] And she continued to ponder their meaning for another twenty years, probing the ultimate mysteries of human experience. The end result was her Long Text of the *Showings*. Julian, a mature lover of Christ, had a multitude of questions; but she never doubted that "love was his meaning."[20]

## HER THEOLOGY
· · · · · · · · · · · · ·

Thomas Merton—monk, person of prayer, and writer who plumbed the depths of God in the twentieth century—named Julian as one of the world's great theologians of all time.[21] And this writer understands why, for Julian is a brilliant, mature, intense lover of God who pondered, probed, and pushed her way into some level of understanding mystery. It is nothing less than "awesome" that a fourteenth-century anchoress could speak so powerfully to today's world. We *know* the power of evil, through the horror of the Holocaust. And while she could say with utter certainty that God is Love, she, too, anguished, "what does that mean in a world that is so saturated with sin and suffering?" In faith seeking understanding, we honor human experience and begin to name God in ways that reflect that experience. So did she. For she described the motherhood of God in a unique way. And, long before twentieth-century psychologists, she understood that we humans struggle for integration and wholeness. Like many of us, she questioned the role of the church in all this, trying to make sense of the beauty of the Body of Christ and the often-sullied image of that Body's actions in the world. What follows, then, is a brief look at her method, her understanding of Love (who is our beginning and our end), and her overarching theme of human integration. This last includes mention of the nature of God and humanity, the nature of sin, the necessity of healing, and the role of the church in all this, according to Julian.

Her approach or method is in line with the monastic tradition, rather than the medieval scholastics.[22] She offers three means to honor God by helping us gain an elementary (she calls it ABC) knowledge of the divine. "The first is the use of [human] natural reason. The second is the common teaching of Holy Church. The third is the inward grace-giving operation of the Holy Spirit; and these three are all from one God. God is the foundation of our natural reason; and God is the teaching of Holy Church, and God is the Holy Spirit, and they are all different gifts," which God wants us to use well.[23] The teaching of Holy Church includes scripture and tradition.

Julian understands that Love is our beginning and end. She opens her Long Text in this way, "This is a revelation of love which Jesus Christ, our endless bliss, made in sixteen showings . . . with many fair revelations and teachings of endless wisdom and love, in which all the revelations which follow are founded and connected."[24] And she ends by proclaiming that Christ's meaning was love. "Who reveals it to you? Love. What did he reveal to you? Love. Why does he reveal it to you?

For love. Remain in this, and you will know more of the same. But you will never know different, without end."[25] But she is not content to bask in the glow of this knowledge, for there is too much pain in the world. So it becomes very clear to her, as she sees in her visions, that the measure of Love is Christ's Passion. For Jesus assures her, "It is a joy, a bliss, an endless delight to me that ever I suffered my Passion for you; and if I could suffer more, I should suffer more."[26] Indeed, it is this intense love which creates in the first place, which keeps everything—even a little hazelnut—in existence, and which heals the wounds of our lives into badges of honor. But, as Julian observes, it is hard to comprehend this much love; for "some of us believe that God is almighty and may do everything, and that [God] is all wisdom and can do everything, but that [God] is all love and wishes to do everything, there we fail."[27] She concludes, "And so I saw most surely that it is quicker for us and easier to come to the knowledge of God than it is to know our own soul. For our soul is so deeply grounded in God and so endlessly treasured that we cannot come to knowledge of it until we first have knowledge of God, who is the Creator to whom it is united."[28]

So Julian spent a lifetime longing for, responding to, and probing this God "who is almighty, all wise and all good."[29] She saw that "God wishes to be known";[30] and she opened herself wholeheartedly. "God, of your goodness give me yourself, for you are enough for me, and I can ask for nothing which is less which can pay you full worship."[31] And God showed her the Passion of Christ; "in the same revelation, suddenly the Trinity filled my heart full of the greatest joy. . . . For the Trinity is God, God is the Trinity. The Trinity is our maker, the Trinity is our protector, the Trinity is our everlasting lover, the Trinity is our endless joy and our bliss, by our Lord Jesus Christ and in our Lord Jesus Christ."[32] Delving ever more deeply into this love, she saw this: "God almighty is our loving Father, and God all wisdom is our loving Mother, with the love and goodness of the Holy Spirit, which is all one God, one Lord."[33] It was God's "eternal purpose to create human nature . . . by full agreement of the whole Trinity"[34] so that together we might praise, thank, and delight in God. She saw that the Trinity continues to work in us through Christ, to restore, heal, and make us whole. And this led her to a unique reflection on the Motherhood of God.

Until Julian, there were only hints and snatches of this divine motherhood. Certainly, scripture points in this direction.[35] And the eleventh-century theologian Anselm of Canterbury spoke of Jesus as Mother, laboring on the Cross for us, healing our wounds.[36] Also, twelfth-century Cistercian spirituality saw God as a patient and nurturing mother.[37] But, in her Long Text, Julian develops this to a fuller extent than ever before. "I understand three ways of contemplating motherhood in God. The first is the foundation of our nature's creation; the second is his taking of our nature, where the motherhood of grace begins; the third is the motherhood at work."[38] And Jesus is true motherhood at work. While some earthly mothers fall short, "our true Mother Jesus alone bears us for joy and for endless life."[39] For Jesus labored for us on the cross, and "feeds us with himself . . . and with all the sweet sacraments he sustains us most mercifully and graciously."[40] So it is that true mother church, at its very core, is Mother Jesus.

But, how does she understand humanity? Julian saw that those who are saved are God's noblest creation. "Our soul is a created trinity, like the uncreated blessed Trinity, known and loved from without beginning, and in the creation united to the Creator."[41] Indeed, "our nature is wholly in God."[42] Like Christ, we are a mixture of God's substance and human sensuality, "our ordinary physical and psychological life."[43] But he was the *begotten* Son and we are created. Unlike Christ, our sensuality can become focused on other than God. It is then that we become broken and fragmented, out of sync with God, self, and one another. It is then that we become twisted or distorted. It is then that sin enters the picture. Julian was troubled in all this, even though God showed her that "sin has no kind of substance, no share in being, nor can it be recognized except by the pain caused by it."[44] Indeed, God had assured her that "all will be well."[45] But, it seemed to her "that it was impossible that every kind of thing should be well,"[46] given the existence of sin. God then revealed to her the parable of the Lord and the servant, which she pondered for years.[47] She came to understand that God is the Lord, who is so connected to us that God waits for us in the wilderness until Christ, the ultimate servant, has won us over. It is Christ, the wounded One, who heals our wounds so that they become badges of honor. It is Christ who still thirsts for us, longing for us to turn with contrition and focus our loving attention on God, rather than our stumbling. It is Christ who assures that our tested faith, sin and all, is worth more than a naïve faith that never struggles. For "we are his joy and his delight, and he is the remedy of our life."[48]

Since the true church is Mother Jesus, the church plays a most important role in this healing process. Julian saw that God does not blame us for sin, for "our good Lord Jesus [has] taken upon him all our blame."[49] And yet, it is our fixation on other than God that needs healing. So God desires our "longing and desiring," our turning back to God.[50] The true church, in its wisdom, understands that by "contrition we are made clean, by compassion we are made ready, and by true longing for God we are made worthy. . . . For every sinful soul must be healed by these medicines."[51] Indeed, as Grace Jantzen says so powerfully: "It is just this that is the primary task of the church: mediating the love of God to broken men and women so that they may find deliverance from their sinfulness and healing for their wounds."[52] It is only then that church becomes Mother Jesus.

"Here end the sublime and wonderful revelations of the unutterable love of God, in Jesus Christ vouchsafed to a dear lover of his, and in her to all his dear friends and lovers whose hearts like hers do flame in the love of our dearest Jesus."[53]

## SOME RESOURCES

Baker, Denise Nowakowski. *Julian of Norwich's Showings: From Vision to Book.* Princeton, NJ: Princeton University Press, 1994.

Jantzen, Grace. *Julian of Norwich: Mystic and Theologian.* Mahwah, NJ: Paulist Press, New edition, 2000.

Julian of Norwich. *Showings, The Classics of Western Spirituality,* trans. from the critical text with an introduction by Edmund Colledge, O.S.A. and James Walsh, S.J. New York and Ramsey, Toronto: Paulist Press, 1978.

Nuth, Joan M. *Wisdom's Daughter: The Theology of Julian of Norwich.* New York: Crossroad, 1991.

Pelphrey, Brant. *Christ Our Mother: Julian of Norwich.* London: Darton, Longman and Todd, 1989.

## NOTES

1.  Grace Jantzen, *Julian of Norwich: Mystic and Theologian* (Mahwah, NJ: Paulist Press, New edition, 2000), p. 7; hereafter referred to as Jantzen. She makes reference here to David Knowles and Dimitri Obolensky, *The Christian Centuries: Vol. II The Middle Ages* (London: Darton, Longman & Todd, and New York: Paulist Press, 1969), p. 57.

2.  Julian of Norwich, *Showings,* translated from the critical text with an introduction by Edmund Colledge, O.S.A. and James Walsh, S.J. (New York and Ramsey, Toronto: Paulist Press, 1978), Long Text (hereafter called LT) 27, p. 225; hereafter referred to as Julian.

3.  They originated in the Low Countries during the High Middle Ages and combined a life of prayer and social action.

4.  Eileen Powers, *Medieval English Nunneries c.1275 to 1535* (London: Hafner Publishing and New York: Biblo & Tannen, 1922; reprinted by permission of Cambridge University Press, 1964), p. 238, as found in Jantzen, p. 18.

5.  See Romans 6:3-5.

6.  Jantzen, p. 28.

7.  Ibid.

8.  Ibid., p. 33.

9.  *The Ancrene Riwle VIII*, ed. James Morton (London: Chatto and Windus, and Boston: John W. Luce, 1907), p. 319; hereafter noted as AR, as found in Jantzen, p. 34.

10. Ibid.

11. Jantzen, p. 40.

12. AR, p. 293, as found in Jantzen, p. 42.

13. Jantzen, p. 47.

14. Julian, LT 2, pp. 177-178.

15. Ibid.

16. Julian, LT 2, p. 179.

17. Julian, LT 1, p. 175.

18. Ibid., pp. 175-177.

19. This became known as the Short Text of the *Showings*.

20. Julian, LT 86, p. 342.

21. Thomas Merton, *Conjectures of a Guilty Bystander* (Garden City, NY: Doubleday, 1966), pp. 191-192, as found in Jantzen, p. 90.

22. On page 104, Grace Jantzen relies on a work by Dom Jean Leclercq to contrast the monastic tradition, which relies on reason, scripture, and tradition, with the medieval scholastic method, which downplayed human experience.

23. Julian, LT 80, p. 335. Note that it is the *teaching* of Holy Church to which she adheres; and yet, even here, she will question what she does not understand.

24. Julian, LT 1, p. 175.

25. Julian, LT, 86, p. 342.

26. Julian, LT 22, p. 216.

27. Julian, LT 73, p. 323.

28. Julian, LT 56, p. 288.

29. Julian, LT 5, p. 184.

30. Ibid.

31. Ibid.

32. Julian, LT 4, p. 181; her reflection on the Trinity is found at length in her Long Text.

33. Julian, LT 58, p. 293.

34. Ibid.

35. See, for example, Exodus 19:4; Isaiah 42:14; 49:4-15; 66:13; Wisdom 7:25-26; Luke 13:34.

36. Jantzen, p. 118; St. Anselm is the one who defined theology as "faith seeking understanding."

37. Jantzen, p. 117; contemporary theologian Sallie McFague describes God as Mother in her *Models of God*. But her image of mother is lioness of justice as well as nurturing compassion.

38. Julian, LT 59, p. 297.

39. Julian, LT 60, p. 298.

40. Ibid.

41. Julian, LT 55, p. 287.

42. Julian, LT 57, p. 291.

43. Jantzen, p. 147. This is not a body/soul dichotomy; rather, it takes account of God's breath in our flesh.

44. Julian, LT 27, p. 225.

45. Julian, LT 63, p. 305.

46. Julian, LT 32, p. 233.

47. This is described in more detail in the liturgy itself. Also, consider the similarity to the Good Samaritan parable, Luke 10:25-37. What if Jesus is the one in the ditch, waiting for compassion?

48. Julian, LT 79, p. 335.

49. Julian, LT 51, p. 275; this is part of the parable of the Lord and the servant.

50. Julian, LT 51, p. 276.

51. Julian, LT 39, p. 245.

52. Jantzen, p. 199.

53. Julian, LT 86, p. 343. This is the very last sentence of her Long Text.

# twelve

# T HE MADRES OF THE

# PLAZA DE MAYO

# Our Pain Is Transformed Into Power for Good by Wisdom

........................................................

*Greeters welcome everyone and offer a "diaper" or white cloth to each person, along with the program and an 8.5" x 11" sheet of paper. These white cloths and papers will be used during the ritual. The focus of the worship setting is a table, covered with some white cloths. On the table are the scriptures and a large picture of one of the Madres of the Plaza de Mayo in Argentina.*

*Ministers:   leader, narrator, five voices, cantor, and musicians*

*Materials:   table, a "diaper" or white cloth, 8.5" x 11" sheet of paper, scripture, a large picture of one of the Madres (or an Argentinean woman of their age)[1]*

## Introductory Rites

.............................................................

CALL TO WORSHIP                                          *Please stand*
. . . . . . . . . . . . . . . . . . .

Leader:     Wisdom is a street preacher,
            raising her voice,
            crying out "to all that live,"[2]
            taking her stand at the city gates.

All:        "Hear, for I will speak noble things" . . .
            I will speak truth . . . and all that "is right."[3]

Leader:     For "wickedness is an abomination" to her lips;[4]
            evil, pride, and arrogance she cannot abide.
            Yes, Wisdom walks "in the way of righteousness,
            along the paths of justice."[5]

All:        Insistent, persistent, she is not to be ignored.
             Listen! Take heed! And walk the path of life!

## OPENING HYMN

"On Holy Ground," text and tune by Donna Peña, GIA Publications, Inc., © 1992.

# Liturgy of the Word

PROVERBS 8:1-21                           *Please be seated*

## PSALM 63

"Your Love Is Finer Than Life," text by Marty Haugen (based on Psalm 63), tune by Marty Haugen, GIA Publications, Inc., © 1982.

## THE STORY OF THE MADRES
## OF THE PLAZA DE MAYO *(narrator and five voices)*

*Narrator:*
The story of the Madres of the Plaza de Mayo in Argentina must be told. They are street preachers, too, women of wisdom, with an "in your face" style. Their "voice is bold, forthright, challenging" and authentic, true to their own experience.[6] And their message is a simple one. Listen to me! And answer me! "For my mouth will speak utter truth; wickedness is an abomination to my lips."[7] Who are these women? What evil did they denounce? How did they do it, and with what results?

The date is March 24, 1976. The place is Argentina. On that day, "three commanding officers of the armed forces—General Jorge Rafael Videla of the army, Admiral Emilio Eduardo Massera of the navy, and Brigadier Ramon Agosti of the air force—staged a successful coup" and grasped power for themselves by statute.[8] It was the beginning of what came to be known as "the dirty war."[9] It was the beginning of the disappearances, of the dark night of crimes against humanity. In "the middle of the night, or in the hours just before dawn, Ford Falcons without license plates would slide through the street like sharks."[10] Out for blood, the drivers—security guards, sharks themselves—would pillage, rape, violate, destroy a household, emerging—most often—with a young adult, who disappeared.

*Voice 1:*
"My son and his wife were lawyers. When they took him away, she told me not to worry. She would draw up a writ of *habeas corpus*. He would be returned in a few days. The days stretched into weeks. . . . The weeks multiplied and he didn't appear. The days were bearable, but nights I lay there wondering if he was cold. The possibilities created their own darkness. After months passed, his wife left the country. Years slipped by. His wife returned from exile. But he didn't appear, he who devoured new books and passed them on to me. He was so busy helping others he forgot about his own safety. . . ."[11]

*Narrator:*
The disappeared. They were the sons and daughters with a social conscience. Editors and journalists. Doctors and lawyers. Teachers. "Anyone who expressed concern for the poor or—even worse—who tried to unite and empower them."[12] The military junta named them subversives, and named itself savior of the western soul.

*Voice 2:*
"A dense silence descended upon" our "country, the same silence of self-preservation, apathy, and hopelessness that prevailed in Germany while the Nazis were taking away Jews." . . . "The intention was to make all the Argentineans disappear as persons and as citizens."[13] Ultimately, the government after the junta would claim that nine thousand had disappeared, but we Madres continually proclaimed, "No! It's more like thirty thousand, at least—to say nothing of the ripples of agony in family, friends, and loved ones!"[14]

## MUSICAL REFRAIN
• • • • • • • • • • • • • • • •

"Within Our Darkest Night," text by the Taize Community, 1991, tune by Jacques Berthier, Les Presses Taize, GIA Publications, Inc., © 1991.

*Narrator:*
Yes, the spark of prophetic wisdom ignited and found a home in the Madres of the Plaza de Mayo. They were ordinary women, homemakers whose lives revolved around the church, the husband as protector, and their own beloved children. They knew their place in a society that put them on a pedestal—and on the margins. Until the disappearances.

---

First, there was despair and total powerlessness. But then came action. "Where is my child?" The question addressed—again and again—to police stations, prisons, churches, military barracks, any government agency that might know something. One . . . another . . . several . . . many asking that same all-important question. Listen, as one of the Madres tells of their beginnings.

*Voice 3:*
It is April 30, 1977. The place is the Plaza de Mayo. It is the place of revolution, where we declared our independence from Spain in 1816. It is the place of power. The cathedral's spires tower at one end, the Casa Rosada, or presidential palace, guards the other end, with commercial and government buildings in between. We are in the Plaza de Mayo for the first time. Fourteen of us, watching over our shoulders, carrying only bus fare and identity cards—no purse—just in case the police come, and we have to make a run for it. It is Azucena who suggests it. She has unbounded energy and ideas, with a smile that radiates confident compassion. We found each other at the Ministry of the Interior, taken in by the woman there who had been so friendly . . . until we realized we were being watched. Now we meet at Azucena's house, or in one of the few churches that still welcomes us. But, as Azucena says, "it's time to go to the Casa Rosada. It's time to talk to the president!" We are so nervous that day that we forget it is a Saturday! Nobody is there for us to see! But, on that day, we begin to claim holy ground. Within us, the process of replacing fear with prophetic wisdom. And, around us, we stake a claim to the Plaza de Mayo as our very own.

*Narrator:*
Yes, you gather there now every Friday afternoon, drawing in more and more Madres, confidently claiming your space for truth-telling. You see the president, but to no avail. "What do the writs of *habeas corpus* say? They are not detained. Well, then, they are not detained."[15] When the police use force to scatter you, you begin to walk, counterclockwise in defiance, two by two around that great Plaza. And in September of that year, you don your symbol as you walk, a white shawl, a baby diaper, with your child's name written on it, in holy script.

*Voice 4:*
You chose white
because you refuse to mourn.
Your scarves illuminate
the stained streets, the steps of the subway,

the bus depots with their tired passengers.
You wear white to confound the enemy,
to be distinguished in a crowd, your white wings
scudding ahead of the racing ocean.
Your pañuelos carry the wisdom
of the household, of two hands becoming twelve,
the multiplication of loaves and fishes.
Tied together, they make a cordon
to protect your young helpers from the police.
They surround a paddy wagon with a Mother inside. . . .
You chose white, the milky sky
before dawn. You chose as your uniforms,
a simple diaper, a baby-shawl.[16]

## MUSICAL REFRAIN
· · · · · · · · · · · · · · · ·

"Stand Firm," arrangement Iona Community, © 1998 WGRG (Wild Goose Resource Group). Found in *There Is One Among Us*, GIA Publications, Inc.

*Narrator:*
You became transformed from victims to self-confident truth tellers. And yet, there were some—even supporters—who would back away from you, in fear for their lives. But, even when you were infiltrated and Azucena became one of the disappeared, you kept coming. You did the unimaginable. You raised a voice never heard before in Argentina. You "forged a set of democratic and humane values out of" your "own searing experiences in the search for" your "disappeared" children.[17] You brought your message before the world community as early as 1978, during two major events held that year in Argentina: the World Cup soccer matches and the International Conference on Cancer Research. You formed networks throughout Argentina—and the world. You became an association on August 22, 1979, and you won the support of human rights groups worldwide. You traveled. And you won the personal support of President Pertini of Italy, but you had a much more difficult time with the pope. In 1979 you could not get an audience with him in Rome, but a Uruguayan bishop was able to get you up front as he went by. You thrust the pictures of your children into his hands, but he let them fall to the ground, with the words, "There are disappeared in many countries."[18] Eventually, you would talk to him, face to face. And you would learn, so much, in all of this. Listen!

---

*The Madres of the Plaza de Mayo*

*Voice 5:*
After two years of activity, we learned some measure of happiness. We had forged "new ties of affection, serving as a refuge against a society and, in many cases, an extended family that rejected" us.[19]

*Voice 1:*
"Proclaiming the truth in a regime dedicated to systematic lies and cover-ups may have been dangerous, but it was also an important source of power."[20]

*Voice 2:*
"In the most benign political system someone who speaks the truth with clarity and simplicity will offend many people."[21] It is the price of bringing about justice.

*Voice 3:*
We have chosen to feel the pain of others and to keep our wounds open in order to stay focused on our cause. We have chosen not to accept the government's law, which presumes the death of our children; for we have chosen to keep alive their hopes for reform and for a world without injustice or exploitation.[22] We have chosen to be one with those who suffer injustice.

*Voice 4:*
Our motherhood has been turned inside out. "Our children begot us. You stop being a conventional mother when you give birth to children who think or work for something beyond their narrow personal goals."[23]

*Voice 5:*
We have learned courage, by "a road that is neither easy nor comfortable. It is dignified, and life has no meaning without dignity, without justice, without liberty, and without love." We have learned that "to live is to struggle and to struggle is to dream."[24]

*Narrator:*
Yes, you are Wisdom's prophets. With a style as bold and as brash as that of the Wisdom Woman herself. And, just like her, you had your critics. Some said you were too easily taken in by radical groups with their own agenda. Others said you remained too focused on motherhood. Still others called you anarchists; for you dreamed of a radical future with equality for all—something Argentina had never known—

without offering a plan, or a structure for how this might happen. But, that was not your gift. Your divine spark that ignited the globe was nothing less than this. A way of life, a new way of love, "based upon equality and ties of affection among its members."[25] Truth telling to power, regardless of the cost. And, motherhood that is big enough for all. As you put it,

*Voices 1-5:*
"All mothers, one mother. All children, one child."[26]

## MUSIC

"Stand Firm," noted earlier, with verses (O my sisters, stand very firm, etc).

# Ritual of Walking the Path of Prophetic Wisdom

## INVITATION *(Leader)*

Each of us has heard Wisdom's call. Each of us has a fire, a divine spark, that Wisdom has kindled within us. Each of us has a piece of the truth that is emblazoned on our hearts, born out of the searing experience of our lives. It is a piece of the truth that we are now invited to name and to claim. Take a moment, in the silence, to reflect upon, name, and write down on your sheet of paper that piece of truth. Then, we will each be invited to put on the shawl and walk around, counterclockwise, two by two, in silence, holding the statement of our truth. It might have to do with parenting, with health care, with the prison system, with our experience of church, with whatever has become a passion in our lives.

*Silence*

## BLESSING OF THE WHITE SHAWLS

*The leader encourages each person to follow her lead in silently lifting up the shawl—a symbol of prophetic truth telling in solidarity with all who suffer—for God's blessing. During this time the instrumental music of "Pues Si Vivivos" ("If We Are Living," see below) softly begins.*

PROCESSION OF PROPHETIC WISDOM

*Each person is invited to walk in twos, counterclockwise, around the circumference of the worship space. During this time, the following hymn is sung by the musicians, first in Spanish, then in English.*

MUSIC

"Pues Si Vivivos" ("If We Are Living"), text is traditional Spanish (based on Romans 14:8), translation by Deborah L. Schmitz, GIA Publications, Inc., © 1994. Tune is traditional Spanish, arr. by Diana Kodner, GIA Publications, Inc., © 1994.

## Closing Rites

BLESSING                                                    *Please stand*

Leader:      We have become a blessing, in solidarity with Wisdom and the Madres of the Plaza de Mayo. Let us now turn to our walking partner and bless one another in whatever way seems appropriate.

CLOSING HYMN

"God, Whose Purpose Is to Kindle," text by David E. Trueblood, © 1967, tune is Beethoven's "Hymn to Joy."

NOTES

1.    Many such photos can be found in Marguerite Guzman Bouvard, *Revolutionizing Motherhood: The Mothers of the Plaza de Mayo* (Wilmington, DE: A Scholarly Resources Inc. Imprint, 1994); hereafter referred to as Bouvard.

2.    See Proverbs 8:4.

3.    See Proverbs 8:6, 7a.

4.    See Proverbs 8:7b.

5.    See Proverbs 8:20.

6.    Bouvard, p. 251.

7.    See Proverbs 8:7.

8.  Bouvard, p. 19.

9.  The "dirty war" referred to the rape, torture, and murder of the disappeared under the military junta. This junta fell from power in 1983, in some measure due to the efforts of the Madres. On December 10, 1983—Human Rights Day—the new president, Raul Alfonsin, was inaugurated. He pledged human justice, but the military continued to pressure this new government. In the end, a number of the military leaders responsible for the "dirty war" were exonerated. Also, some of the Madres, in a desire to work with the new government, formed a new organization in 1986; the remainder continued to press for answers to the disappearances and for a more equal and just society.

10. Bouvard, p. 24.

11. Bouvard, telling Josefa's dream, p. 18.

12. Bouvard, p. 37.

13. Ibid., p. 43.

14. This information is found in Bouvard, p. 31.

15. Bouvard, p. 70.

16. Poem, "A White Shawl," found in Bouvard, p. 64.

17. Bouvard, p. 59.

18. Ibid., pp. 88-89.

19. Ibid., p. 93.

20. Ibid., p. 95.

21. Ibid., p. 108. This is descriptive of Hebe de Bonafini, president of the Madres.

22. Bouvard, pp. 151-152.

23. Ibid., p. 178.

24. Ibid., p. 185. The quote is actually taken from a group of their young supporters, referring to the Madres.

25. Bouvard, p. 219.

26. This captures the essence of their work.

# The Wisdom Woman in the Book of Proverbs . . . and Beyond

When I first delved into the story of the Madres, several women in scripture came to mind. Surely the Madres were like the Canaanite woman, who refused to leave Jesus alone until he healed her daughter (Matthew 15:21-28). Or the persistent widow, who insistently cried out for justice (Luke 18:1-8). Or, the mother of the seven martyred brothers in the Second Book of Maccabees, whose nobility and courage surpassed even that of her sons (2 Maccabees 7:1-41). And then I encountered the Wisdom Woman of Proverbs 8:1-21, once again. The street preacher. *She* was the one. She fit their spirit. For, just as personified Wisdom emerged out of a time of gut-wrenching loss, the passion of the Madres flared out of their searing experience of terror and grief. And the Madres, like the Wisdom Woman, proclaimed their truth unceasingly and openly, at the place of judgment, the city gates (of the Plaza de Mayo). They remained women rooted in family and home, like personified Wisdom, but their home and family would become the world stage. They were no longer simply the mothers of their own children, but of all children who were "disappeared" in any way. Theirs was a message of justice that their society and church could not ignore. And, as it turned out, theirs was a message that could only be embodied in a woman, when the fear of oppression had made God seem very distant from the lives of many ordinary people. Finally, in light of September 11, 2001, the persistence of the Madres, like the Wisdom Woman, to walk the path of justice, is a story for our day.[1] With that said, it's time to explore the Wisdom Woman.

We first encounter her in the Book of Proverbs. She is Wisdom Woman, crying out in the streets, at the busiest corner, raising her voice in the public square, proclaiming her message at the city gates, the place of judgment.[2] She is Wisdom Woman, comfortable in the public domain. She is determined to judge and be judged by what she has to say: it is only through her that people find life, insight, prudence, understanding, fear of the Lord, and true wealth and happiness.[3] She is complex, a multi-faceted expression of Israelite faith at a traumatic time. For she arrives in early post-exilic Palestine, around the second quarter of the fifth century, B.C.E. (before the Common Era). The people of Israel have just returned from exile in Babylon, distraught with the destruction of their key religious symbols of Temple and King. Displacement is everywhere and cuts across religious, political, economic, and social lines. What meaning are they to find in all this? Who will offer them hope?

In the Hebrew canon, the Wisdom Woman is only to be found in the Book of Proverbs.[4] For Roman Catholics, she is also found in the Deuterocanonical Books of Baruch, Ecclesiasticus (or The Wisdom of

Jesus son of Sirach), and the Wisdom of Solomon.[5] Her Greek name is Sophia, the English transliteration of the Greek word for wisdom. Some prefer her by this name; it is more personal, they say, someone to be experienced, rather than an object to be kept at a distance. Regardless of how she is named, Wisdom Woman/Sophia remains a mystery, unfinished, raising more questions than answers. Is she originally a divine being? Yahweh's own wisdom? The tradition of the teachers or sages? The Proverb collection itself? Is she the voice of world order? A Cosmic Guide? Is she God? Or a bridge between God and humanity?[6]

Personified Wisdom, especially as found in the Book of Proverbs, will be briefly explored here: her origin out of the experience of the returning exiles and the tradition available to Israelites, her function as both a literary device and religious symbol, and her cry to us today for further development.

## EXPERIENCE OF THE ISRAELITES:
## THE CONTEXT OF EARLY POST-EXILIC ISRAEL

Most scholars date the final editing of Proverbs in the second quarter of the fifth century, B.C.E. For this book reveals contact with the book of Malachi, written about the same time. There is a similar social setting, and similar religious and social abuses are named. In particular, there was displacement of devastating proportions; the exiles returned to a Palestine that was markedly different from the one they had left behind. Samaritans had greater influence in the north; and other peoples had moved onto land in the south. There were struggles around land claims, family structure, and the issue of foreign influence and "foreign" wives. Tensions and abuses were everywhere to be found: oppression of the poor by the rich, acquisition of land by divorcing native wives to marry "foreign" wives, and worship abuses by offering offensive sacrifices, to name a few.[7] Above all, the "throne of God's anointed was not just empty but destroyed."[8] And the king had been a mediator of the divine, at least in the ideal. Politically, adjustment to these new circumstances began to take the form of a governing group of 150 Jewish males, largely responsible for the resettlement of the people. On the religious level, there was an increasing reliance on a written tradition, rather than an oral one. And, with such seismic shifts in everyday life, the seeds of apocalyptic thought began to germinate.[9] But, who could replace the king, especially when God seemed so distant? What was embedded in the Jewish tradition that could offer hope, in a new way?

## THE TRADITION:
## FAMILY AND THE ROLE OF WOMEN
● ● ● ● ● ● ● ● ● ● ● ● ● ● ● ● ● ● ● ● ● ● ● ● ● ● ● ● ● ● ● ● ●

Before the kingdom, the *bet-ab*, or "the father's house," had been the primary source of political, economic, and social authority, as well as the locus of Israelite values and relationship with God. Generally speaking, this *bet-ab* comprised an extended, intergenerational family. After the exile, there was a return to the authority of this family system. Indeed, on an unofficial level, the family had always remained an important source of values. Now it was possible to turn to the God who is Creator and Parent, whose presence is to be found in the "stuff" of everyday life.

And, in the realm of family life, the woman was significant, even in a patriarchal system. According to Claudia Camp, scattered evidence reveals "an explicit inclusion of the women in the economic, religious and political spheres" of life after the exile.[10] For example, both creation accounts of Genesis, edited in their final form around this time, proclaim equality between woman and man.[11] Probably everything but the priesthood and participation in the council of 150 families was open to women.

Indeed, as Camp points out, women continually exercised positions of power and authority within the context of the household. Potentially, a woman was counselor to her husband, and manager—even builder—of the household. The power she wielded was often indirect, sometimes even manipulative. Also, she prepared the meals, sometimes even hosting lavish feasts, if she was wealthy enough.[12] She was a lover, engaged in the process of seeking and finding her beloved. And such love could be the source of her strength, for love "is strong as death, passion fierce as the grave. Its flashes are flashes of fire, a raging flame."[13] Finally, she passed on the tradition of her people, as teacher of her children. In all this, she became the embodiment of "wisdom, that most practical of religious traditions."[14]

Yes, wisdom took on flesh in so many women. Rebekah (Genesis 27:1-28:9). Tamar (Genesis, chapter 38), Shiphrah, and Puah (Exodus 2:1-10). The women around the birth of Moses—his mother Jochebed and sister Miriam—and Pharaoh's daughter (Exodus 2:1-10). Ruth and Naomi (The Book of Ruth). Michal, a wife of David (1 Samuel 19:11-17). And Esther (Book of Esther), among others. They seized the indirect means of power available to them to further the work of God and set God's people free, often upsetting the established order to forge a new way. Some were bold and even aggressive, such as Shiphrah, and

Puah, the women around the birth of Moses, and Tamar and Ruth. Others, like Rebekah and Esther, accomplished their plan with a feast. It is not far-fetched to maintain that all of these were house builders— of the house of Israel. Still others were prophetic, crying out for justice at the city gates, stretching out the hand toward another, as in the case of Tamar. A few were explicitly named prophetesses, for it was the norm in Israel to call in a "divinely gifted individual" to authenticate the written tradition.[15] And Huldah the prophetess (2 Kings 22:14-20) was just such a person. Finally, there were wise women of Israel, like Deborah (Judges, chapters 4 and 5), the wise woman of Tekoa (2 Samuel 14), and the wise woman of Abel (2 Samuel 20) who represented unusual but powerful examples of women's leadership.

## WISDOM WOMAN AS A
## LITERARY DEVICE AND RELIGIOUS SYMBOL

Onto this stage strides the Wisdom Woman. She "works," she "takes hold" of the popular imagination because she is embedded in the tradition. She is, as Wisdom personified, a literary device first of all, according to Camp. Personification is "a manner of speech endowing things with life," personalizing the impersonal.[16] Personification points to the here and now, moves us from the specific to the universal, makes generalizations based upon many experiences of wisdom, and creates a poetic surplus of meaning.

But, she is strong enough to become a religious symbol, as well. A symbol is an action or event which points beyond itself to the deeper meaning of life. And religion has been defined as a system of sacred symbols which "function to synthesize a people's ethos: the tone, character, and quality of their life, its moral and aesthetic style and mood; and their world view: the picture they have of the way things in sheer actuality are, their most comprehensive ideas of order."[17] Wisdom Woman points beyond herself to tradition, to Yahweh, the one true source of Israel's values, and to everyday life on the street, at the gate, in the home, and in love relationships. In bridging the divide between God and everyday life, she theologically unites human and divine. And she does this precisely as woman, in ways familiar to the tradition. If the household (or *bet-ab*) is the place of God's blessing, the poet of Proverbs presents the wise wife as the source of the household's identity (Proverbs 31:21, 27). She builds her house (the house of Israel) and sets a feast there, boldly proclaiming that this is the very place where life—God's supreme gift—is to be found (Proverbs 9:1-6). She is also a counselor, the one who authorizes human government (Proverbs 8:15-16). She is even the intimate of God at the dawn of creation, God's First-Born, playmate and artisan, "delighting in the human race" (Proverbs 8:22-31).[18] It is this woman who now defines society, for "her works praise her in the city gates" (Proverbs 31:31, the final statement of this Book). Why a woman? God was distant—or so it seemed—and this new mediator could point to God in the midst of the everyday experience. As religious symbol, she was capable of bringing people's worldview together with their way of life, offering them divine/human congruency.

One final point must be made regarding Wisdom Woman as a religious symbol. It must be said that the religious tradition of Israel was never immune from the traditions of its neighbors. Certainly, there is evidence of goddess traditions at work within the final composite of this Wisdom Woman. Scholars definitely find the influence of Ma'at, the Egyptian goddess of justice, at work in two poems. Just as Ma'at is the foundation of Pharaoh's throne, so Wisdom Woman can proudly proclaim, "By me kings reign, and rulers decree what is just; by me rulers rule, and nobles, all who govern rightly."[19] And, just as Ma'at is both the child of the creator and the creator's plan itself, so Wisdom is the Creator's First-Born and artisan of creation (Proverbs 8:22-31). Finally, and especially in the deuterocanonical works of Sirach and Wisdom, Wisdom praises herself in ways that are reminiscent of Hellenistic praise of the goddess Isis.

## WISDOM WOMAN IN THE
## BOOKS OF SIRACH AND WISDOM

Are we any closer to naming this Woman's identity? For the Hebrews, who firmly believe in a monotheistic God, she could not be divine. Indeed, personification of wisdom does not require such belief. But, she is clearly an image of God, at the very least in the sense that woman is made in God's image. And, there are some tantalizing hints of divinity that are more fully developed in the deuterocanonical books of Sirach (Ecclesiasticus) and Wisdom. Sirach constructs his book on three great hymns to Wisdom: chapters 1 and 24 and 51:13-30. He suggests that Wisdom came forth "from the mouth of the Most High" (24:3). And when this Word of God sought a "resting place," the "Creator of all" suggested that Wisdom pitch her tent in Israel, specifically in Zion (24:7-10). For Christians, all this will later be suggestive of Jesus. Indeed, in the opening hymn of John's Gospel, it is as though a trumpet announces Jesus as the eternal Word of God, the Logos, who pitched his tent in Israel (John 1:1, 2, 14). The writer of Sirach goes on to describe Wisdom in images from the Hebrew tradition: trees, food, drink, and Torah. Later on, Christians identify these same images with Jesus.

The Book of Wisdom is most clear in suggesting that the Wisdom Woman is divine. "For she is a breath of the power of God, and a pure emanation of the glory of the Almighty. . . . For she is a reflection of eternal light, a spotless mirror of the working of God, and an image of his goodness. Although she is but one, she can do all things, and while remaining in herself, she renews all things; in every generation she passes into holy souls and makes them friends of God, and prophets."[20] In this first century B.C.E. description of Wisdom Woman, she becomes the perfect mirror of God; she has twenty-one attributes in Wisdom 7:22–8:1, the perfect number three multiplied by the perfect number seven.

Some might ask, why does this matter? Here's one view. "A woman whose only symbol for God is male may be able to pray to him and be comforted and strengthened by him, but there is a level which is beyond her reach: she can never identify with him. She may believe that she is created in his image but what does it mean to be like someone who is called 'Father'? Only by denying her own sexuality or by placing it in a sphere which is totally out of reach, beyond sexual identification, can she relate as one who is created in the image of a male god. She can never have the experience that is open to every male in our society: to have her sexual identity affirmed by God, and to identify directly with 'him.'"[21] What do you think?

## THE WISDOM WOMAN AND US
• • • • • • • • • • • • • • • • • • • • • • • • •

It is the position of the authors of *Wisdom's Feast* that the Wisdom Woman remains hidden, decidedly implicit, unfinished, open to becoming more than she is already. "Both in the Hebrew scriptures and in the New Testament, she is cut off or disguised so that her image is never fully formed."[22] In the Hebrew scripture, this is largely the result of being left out of the Hebrew and Protestant canons beyond the Book of Proverbs. How does this happen in the New Testament?

As has already been noted, the Wisdom Woman carries over into the Christian tradition through the person of Jesus. This portrait is most obvious in John's Gospel. Johannine scholar Raymond Brown claims that the Jesus of this Gospel, who is "in the world but not of it," results from "an identification of Jesus with personified divine Wisdom as described in the OT."[23] Jesus is the eternal Word of God, pitching her tent in Israel, calling disciples and crying out for people to choose life, to choose him. Those who do choose him come to know him as Living Water, the Bread of Life, the Light of the World, the True Vine, and Friend. Elsewhere in the New Testament there are a few references to Jesus as personified Wisdom.[24]

And yet, the Wisdom Woman remains veiled. The connections between Jesus and Wisdom Woman have not been made explicit; the lines have not been drawn to connect the dots. Why? The authors of *Wisdom's Feast* conclude that gnosticism and patriarchy are among the reasons for the incomplete development of Wisdom in early Christianity.[25] Because the gnostics—who developed an affinity for the Wisdom tradition— gradually denied the humanity and death of Jesus, the Wisdom tradition lost favor in Christian theology. At the same time, the cultural system of patriarchy gradually reasserted itself into Christian communities by the end of the first century. One need only compare Paul's attitudes on women in Romans 16:1-7, probably written early in the year 58, with those of the person who wrote 1 Timothy 2:8-14, circa 80-90, to get the picture.

What might the future hold for the Wisdom Woman? Elisabeth Schüssler Fiorenza suggests that "Jesus, Miriam's child and Sophia's prophet, goes ahead of us on the open-road to Galilee," still walking Wisdom's path.[26] For her, Jesus proclaims the not yet realized divine vision of a renewed creation, "symbolized in the abundant table set by Divine Wisdom."[27] And, she concludes, the ones who lead us in discipleship today are the women around the globe who struggle for liberation that is rooted in scripture.

## SOME RESOURCES

Camp, Claudia V. *Wisdom and the Feminine in the Book of Proverbs*. Decatur, GA: The Almond Press, Columbia Theological Seminary, 1985.

_____. *Wise, Strange and Holy: The Strange Woman and the Making of the Bible*. Sheffield, England: Sheffield Academic Press, Ltd., 2000.

Cole, Susan, Marian Ronan, and Hal Taussig, editors. *Wisdom's Feast: Sophia in Study and Celebration*. Kansas City: Sheed and Ward, 1996.

Fontaine, Carole R. "Proverbs" in *Women's Bible Commentary, Expanded Edition*. Ed. Carol A. Newsom and Sharon H. Ringe. Louisville, KY: Westminster John Knox Press, 1998, pp. 153-160.

McCreesh, Thomas P., O.P. "Proverbs" in *The New Jerome Biblical Commentary.* Ed. Raymond E. Brown, S.S., Joseph A. Fitzmyer, S.J., and Roland E. Murphy, O. Carm. Englewood Cliffs, NJ: Prentice Hall, 1990, pp. 453-461.

Nowell, Irene. *Women in the Old Testament.* Collegeville, MN: The Liturgical Press, 1997.

## NOTES

• • • • •

1.    For more on the Madres, please read Marguerite Guzman Bouvard, *Revolutionizing Motherhood: The Mothers of the Plaza de Mayo* (Wilmington, DE: Scholarly Resources, Inc., 1994). The author offers many other sources, including newspaper articles, at the end of her book.

2.    See Proverbs 1:20-21.

3.    See the poems that comprise Proverbs 8:1–9:6.

4.    Protestants follow the Hebrew canon for their selection of the Hebrew Scripture or "Old Testament."

5.    Ecclesiasticus and the Wisdom of Solomon were originally written in Greek in the second and first centuries B.C.E., respectively. Baruch, though written originally in Hebrew, now is only preserved in its most ancient form in Greek.

6.    Claudia V. Camp raises most of these questions on pages 217 and 284 of her book *Wisdom and the Feminine in the Book of Proverbs* (Decatur, GA: The Almond Press, Columbia Theological Seminary, 1985); hereafter referred to as Camp.

7.    See Nehemiah 5:1-13 and chapter 13, and Malachi, chapter 2, for example.

8.    Camp, p. 243.

9.    Ibid., p. 243. The word "apocalyptic" derives from the Greek word for revelation. Apocalyptic thought has to do with the expectation of a decisive change in the course of history; God will intervene to create a whole new world. The "in group" understands the work of God in the highly symbolic language; therein lies the hope. It developed ca. 200 B.C.E. and continued through the first century C.E.

10.    Camp, p. 256. See Nehemiah 8:2-3, for example.

11.    See Genesis 1:27. And, in the other creation account (Genesis 2:4–3:24), Phyllis Trible, in her *God and the Rhetoric of Sexuality* (Philadelphia: Fortress Press, 1978), pp. 72-143, describes God's intention as one of equality between man and woman. It is only after eating the fruit that the man begins to dominate.

12. See Esther 5:1-8 and chapter 7, for example.

13. See Song of Solomon 8:6.

14. Camp, p. 147.

15. Ibid., p. 141.

16. Ibid., p. 213.

17. Clifford Geertz, *The Interpretation of Cultures* (New York: Basic Books, p. 89), as found in Camp, p. 229.

18. This poem, Proverbs 8:22-31, has created a scholarly stir. The verb in verse 22, often translated as "created me," might be better translated "conceived me" because verses 24-25 refer to female activity of giving birth. Another translation, a literal one, that is offered by scholars is this: "Yahweh acquired me as the beginning of his way." Finally, the Hebrew in verse 30 has connotations of both "master worker" and "darling child"; both meanings are intended. For information on this, see Carole R. Fontaine, "Proverbs," in *Women's Bible Commentary, Expanded Edition*, Eds. Carol A. Newsom and Sharon H. Ringe (Louisville, KY: Westminster John Knox Press, 1998), p. 156.

19. See Proverbs 8:15-16, part of the larger poem, 8:1-21.

20. See Wisdom 7:25a, b, 26-27.

21. Susan Cole, Marian Ronan, Hal Taussig, *Wisdom's Feast: Sophia in Study and Celebration, New Edition*. Kansas City: Sheed & Ward, 1996, p. 61; hereafter referred to as *Feast*.

22. *Feast*, p. 64.

23. Raymond E. Brown, S.S., *The Gospel According to John, I-XII* (Garden City, NY: Doubleday & Co., 1966), p. CXXII.

24. See Matthew 11:25-27 // Luke 19:21-22, Matthew 11:28-30, Matthew 11:16-19 // Luke 7:31-35, Matthew 23:34-36 // Luke 11:49-51, Matthew 23:37-39 // Luke 13:34-35, 1 Corinthians 1:30, Colossians 1:15-17, Ephesians 3:9-11, James 3:13-17, for example.

25. *Feast*, pp. 43-45.

26. Elisabeth Schüssler Fiorenza, *Jesus: Miriam's Child, Sophia's Prophet* (New York: Continuum, 1994), p. 190. This entire book probes the Jesus tradition in terms of Wisdom.

27. Ibid., p. 189.

# thirteen

MARY OF MAGDALA

# The Truth of Our Lives Must Be Heard

*The scene is a garden, with a large rock near the center. There is a microphone to one side with room for the narrator and several Daughters of Jerusalem. There is a microphone at the center and slightly to the other side. Jesus and Mary will take turns at these microphones. To the other side of the garden is the space for the musicians.*

*Music begins for "Morning Has Broken" as Daughters of Jerusalem, the narrator, and Jesus and Mary come forward. The narrator will assume the leader role during the ritual. Music plays underneath the Call to Worship.*

Ministers:    *Jesus, Mary, several Daughters of Jerusalem, narrator, cantor, and musicians*

Materials:  *whatever is available to create a garden scene*

## Introductory Rites

### CALL TO WORSHIP                  *Please stand*

Leader:    "Set me as a seal upon your heart,
              as a seal upon your arm;

All:       For love is strong as death,
              passion fierce as the grave.

Leader:    Its flashes are flashes of fire, a raging flame.

All:      Many waters cannot quench love,
          neither can floods drown it" (Song of Songs 8:6-7a).

HYMN
• • • • •

"Morning Has Broken," text by Eleanor Farjeon, 1881-1965, *The Children's Bells*, © David Higham Assoc., Ltd.; tune is Bunessan, arr. by Marty Haugen, GIA Publications, Inc.

## Liturgy of the Word
• • • • • • • • • • • • • • • • • • • • • • • • • • • • • • • • • • • • • • •

THE STORY IS TOLD                          *Please be seated*
• • • • • • • • • • • • • • • • • •

Narrator:   A truthful story of Mary of Magdala.

Daughters
of
Jerusalem: Woman, why are you weeping?

Mary:      I weep because I am dark
           and people gaze on me with scorn and taunt me.
           My brothers were angry with me
           and sent me out in the heat of the day
           to care for their vineyard.
           But my own I did not keep.
           I weep because my darkness
           is the darkness of seven demons
           and the last of these is despair
           (Based on Song of Songs 1:5-6; Luke 8:2).

Jesus:     "Arise," Mary, "and come away,
           for now the winter is past,
           the rain is over and gone.
           The flowers appear on the earth;
           the time of singing has come,
           and the voice of the turtledove is heard in our land"
           (from Song of Songs 2:10-12).

Mary:      His voice was sweet;
           and he called me by my name.
           I followed him from Galilee to Jerusalem,
           and my garden—my life—was fragrant with his love.

*(Pause)*

"Awake, O north wind,
and come, O south wind!
Blow upon my garden
that its fragrance may be wafted abroad.
Let my beloved come to his garden"
(from Song of Songs 4:16).

Daughters
of
Jerusalem: Woman, why are you weeping?

Mary: "Now there was a garden in the place where he was crucified, and in the garden there was a new tomb in which no
one had ever been laid. And so, because it was the Jewish
day of preparation, and the tomb was nearby, they laid
Jesus there" (John 19:41-42).

Narrator: Early on the first day of the week, while it was still dark,
Mary Magdalene came to the tomb and saw that the stone
had been removed from the tomb (John 20:1).

Daughters
of
Jerusalem: Woman, why are you weeping?

Mary: "They have taken the Lord out of the tomb,
and we do not know where they have laid him"
(John 20:2b).

Daughters
of
Jerusalem: "Where has your beloved gone,
O fairest among women?
Which way has your beloved turned, that we may seek
him with you?" (Song of Songs 6:1).

Narrator: "But Mary stood weeping outside the tomb"
(John 20:11a).

Jesus: "Woman, why are you weeping?
Whom are you looking for?" (John 20:15a).

Mary: "Sir, you must be the gardener.
If you have carried him away,

tell me where you have laid him,
and I will take him away" (from John 20:15b).

Jesus: "Mary!"

Mary: "Rabbouni!"

Jesus: "Do not hold onto me." Do not cling to the past!
For "I have not yet ascended to the Father.
But go to my brothers and say to them,
'I am ascending to my Father and your Father,
to my God and your God'" (from John 20:17).

Mary: "I have seen the Lord!" I have seen the Lord!
(John 20:18).

Narrator: The Word and Gospel of the Lord.

*Pause*

## MUSICAL REFLECTION
. . . . . . . . . . . . . . . . . . . .

"The Summons," text by John Bell, Iona Community, GIA Publications, Inc., © 1987.

## REFLECTION BY MARY OF MAGDALA
. . . . . . . . . . . . . . . . . . . . . . . . . . . . . .

It's so good to be here today! It's so good to be among people who really *know* me. As a woman healed. Disciple of Jesus. And apostle to the apostles. You know, I can't tell you the number of times I am in a group of people and my name comes up. And you know what happens? Invariably someone raises an eyebrow and says, "Oh, I know *her! She's* the prostitute!" Even though that's nowhere to be found in scripture. And, it keeps on happening. Why, not long ago I met a woman who was certain that I was the woman caught in adultery, even though she was given no name. And in a recent TV program on Jesus there it was again! The same old story! It just keeps following me around.

How did it happen, anyway, that I came to be known as a prostitute, rather than apostle to the apostles? Well, I can tell you this much. Some of the early church fathers started to confuse me with Mary of Bethany. You remember—she's the one who anointed Jesus on his feet. Then they confused us both—and lumped us together—with the "sinful" woman who came in off the streets and wept all over Jesus' feet, then dried them with her hair. Well, guess what? I became that sinful woman. And when someone as powerful as Jerome, early in the fifth century, and Pope Gregory the Great a hundred years later, said it was so, well, then, it *must* be so. Never mind that they were wrong! And artists kept the mistake going down through the centuries.

But *why* did this happen? That's a much harder question to answer, and I really don't know. Were there too many Mary's? Was it easier to put us all together . . . at least, for the person *telling* the story? Or, was it possible that they couldn't—or wouldn't—believe who I *really* was? I don't know. But I do know this. It is *so* important to speak the truth. So *very* important to speak the truth. For if the truth is distorted about any one of us, it will affect every single one of us.

And I know this! I know Jesus. And the power of Jesus over sin, death, demons, and anything and everything that keeps people down. I know . . . because when I met Jesus I was so sick, in every way you can imagine. Are any of you from a small town? Then, you know how it can be when people talk about you. The folks in my hometown of Magdala would whisper about me behind my back . . . *(in a loud whisper) "There she goes, Mary of Magdala, she's full of demons, seven of them."* And I looked it! Jesus must have heard about me, for he knew my name. He called me by name. Ah, but there's the difference. *My name was safe in his mouth.* He spoke my name so tenderly, "Mary . . . Mary." And from that moment on, the demons' lock on me was shattered forever! I looked in his eyes and I saw that *he* believed in *me*, in the strong, charismatic woman I could become. In the powerful preacher I *would* become. And I saw in him my soul mate, the one I would follow anywhere. Throughout all of Galilee, even to Jerusalem.

"Oh, Jerusalem, Jerusalem. . . ." Jesus was brutally murdered there. The man I loved . . . Love itself . . . and hope . . . had been *killed*! I felt like someone had ripped my heart out . . . and there was a gaping hole where my heart used to be. It seemed so final! How could I possibly imagine what God would have in mind? I couldn't. All I could do was stay there . . . and weep. . . . I was in a long line of women, like the women that the prophet Jeremiah had called upon five hundred years earlier when our people could not face the truth about themselves. "Call in the women. Let them weep and wail, long enough and loud enough, so that everyone can finally see the truth: that they had exiled the one true God from their midst."

So I stayed there . . . and I wept . . . until . . . I heard Jesus, the gardener of new creation, call me by my name, in the same way as always,

"Mary." It was *then* that I turned. It was *then* that I knew, it was then that I saw. It was *then* that my tears became the ultimate sacrament of truth, "I have seen the Lord! I have *seen* the *Lord!*" It was Jesus himself who sent me forth, apostle to the apostles. And I have proclaimed that truth ever since, with every fiber of my being.

So, now, I have a question for you. What is the truth you would weep for? Live for? Die for? Love for? What is the truth that grows . . . quickens . . . lives and moves and has its being inside you, readying for the day when you will give it birth? What is the truth that you alone bring here this day?

## Ritual of Truth Telling

Leader: (Invitation to the assembly to name their truth) It takes courage to tell the truth in love. It takes courage to be an apostle, one who is sent by the risen Lord with the truth that is deep inside, that has been reflected upon, that is claimed as one's own, that must be spoken. Take the time you need to reflect upon your truth. It may have to do with parenting or the needs of children; or the needs of older adults, or of the health care system. It may have to do with who we are as church . . . with including everyone, with opening up ordination and/or being more welcoming to those who are homosexual. Whatever it is, it comes out of *your* experience and it is something around which you have passion. Then, as you wish, come forward and name this to one of the leaders (Narrator, Jesus, Mary), who will bless you in your proclamation of this truth.

*"The Summons" is played quietly underneath as people come forward for the following dialogue.*

Leader: _____, what is the truth you wish to proclaim?

Participant: My truth is _____.

Leader: _____, may God grant you courage, love, and wisdom as you are sent forth with this truth.

# Closing Rites

## SENDING FORTH

*Please stand*

Jesus:  "Set me as a seal upon your heart,
as a seal upon your arm;

Mary:  for love is strong as death,
passion fierce as the grave.
Its flashes are flashes of fire, a raging flame.

Both:  Many waters cannot quench love,
neither can floods drown it.

*Pause*

O you who dwell in the gardens,
our companions are listening for your voice;
let us hear it" (from Song of Songs 8:6-7a, 13).

## HYMN

"You Are the Voice," text and tune by David Haas, GIA Publications, Inc., © 1983, 1987.

or

"Shake Up the Morning," text and tune by John L. Bell, Iona Community, GIA Publications, Inc., © 1987.

# Mary of Magdala: Apostle to the Apostles

Will the real Mary of Magdala please stand up? In Eastern Christianity, Mary of Magdala is known as "Apostle to the Apostles," following scripture and the writings of Origen (d. 254 C.E.) and St. John Chrysostom (d. 407 C.E.). But in the West, Mary has trod a very different . . . and conflicted . . . path. Mention her name in any group and invariably someone will identify her as "prostitute," "repentent sinner," and the like. Why? What does scripture say of her? And the Tradition in the West? And why is this important today?

_Mary of Magdala_                                                                    219

Mary of Magdala is named twelve times in this way in the four canoni-cal Gospels—identified by her hometown—and two more times simply as Mary (in John's resurrection account, where she has *just* been identified by her hometown). Additionally, her presence as one of the "pray-ers" in the Upper Room is presumed in Acts 1:14, as one of the "certain women" of Luke 8:2, who followed Jesus from Galilee. Her name appears more than any other woman in the New Testament, except for Mary, the mother of Jesus. Furthermore, whenever Mary is named with other women, her name comes first (except in John's account of the women "standing near the cross of Jesus," where his mother is named first). Scholars generally conclude that she was a leader among the women (in a relational rather than hierarchical way), that she was uniformly known by her hometown roots, and that she "was so prominent a member of the early Christian church that it was impossi-ble for writers to eliminate her name from the resurrection narratives."[1] While all four Gospel writers focus on Mary's role during the Passion and resurrection events, Mark and Luke also mention that Jesus had cast seven demons out of her (Mark 16:9, Luke 8:2). In their day, this meant severe and/or continuing illness, *not* sin. One contemporary scholar suggests that her demons may have included "depression, fear, low self-esteem, doubts, procrastination, bitterness, and self-pity."[2] All the Gospel writers locate Mary of Magdala at the cross (though Luke includes her among "the women who had followed him from Galilee," 23:49) and at the empty tomb (either alone, as in John's Gospel, or with a variety of women, as in the synoptics). And all but Luke name Mary (in Matthew, she is accompanied by "the other Mary") as the first to encounter the risen Jesus.[3] But it is the powerfully poetic John (20:1-2, 11-18) who places this encounter in the garden, evoking memories of the first creation (Mary "mistakes" Jesus for the gardener—of new cre-ation) and the lover seeking her beloved in the Song of Songs. "Where *is* he?!" Mary is the first to know. She turns . . . at the sound of the Good Shepherd calling her by name, to become the first disciple of the risen Jesus. She sees . . . as the first authentic witness to Easter, "I have seen the Lord!"[4] She is sent by the risen Jesus to his siblings[5] with the Good News of Easter. Thus, she is "apostle to the apostles," her identi-ty to this day in the Eastern Christian church.

A very different picture of Mary slowly emerged in the West. In the second century she was still regarded as a leader. Indeed, the non-canonical Gospel of Mary (Magdalene), written in the second century but lost to us from the fourth to the end of the nineteenth century, speaks of Mary as a model disciple. She understood the teaching of Jesus about the seed of the divine within and was teacher to the other disciples. In fact, her spirituality was so respected that she was a source of irritation to Peter, revealing a possible conflict between her followers and those of Peter.[6] In the second and third centuries, she was generally either honored or ignored. But then, slowly, a conflation occurred. Her identity gradually became blurred together with that of Mary of Bethany, who anointed the feet of Jesus (John 12:1-8) and the unnamed "sinful" woman who washed the feet of Jesus with her tears and dried them with her hair (Luke 7:36-50). Generally speaking, the fathers of the Western church preferred one anointing and associated it with Mary, regardless of what was to be found in scripture. Early in the fifth century, the influential Jerome contributed to this conflation, and it was complete by the time of Pope Gregory the Great (c. 540-604 C.E.). But Mary not only represented three women; she came to embody women . . . or more precisely, the conflicted attitudes of the fathers to women. In her resided "the paradoxical ideas of the feminine as the source and destroyer of life, as the dangerous but fascinating seducer of men, as the pure spirit, Sophia-Wisdom."[7] In the Middle Ages, the tradition of Mary, repentant sinner, was filled out with eleventh- and twelfth-century legends of Mary from southern France.[8] She was said to have cured blindness and other ills and to have freed prisoners. At some point, these legends were further conflated with those of Mary of Egypt, a woman who spent thirty years in the desert, clothed only in her hair. Shrines and devotions to this composite Mary of Magdala flourished in the Middle Ages.

And this tradition has continued, down to the present day. Consider the penitent prostitute of both *Jesus Christ Superstar* and *The Last Temptation of Christ*. Consider also a 1988 art exhibit on Mary of Magdala organized by the Petrarch Museum at Fontaine-de-Vaucluse. In a catalogue describing the exhibit it was said, "She [Mary] is still dangerous—a temptress—an object of desire . . . in her woman's body she affirms the power of her femininity. This has the corrupting power of temptation . . . Magdalene of sin, red with the blood of shame, the antithesis of White Mary the mother of God."[9] It is worth noting that one scholar, writing in 1925, recognized the "historical truth" of the scriptural Mary; yet he named the "confusion" in the Tradition as "harmless."[10]

## MARY OF MAGDALA'S SIGNIFICANCE TODAY

Is the confusing and conflicted path that Mary trod in the Western Tradition *really* harmless? Consider this. The church is *still* debating whether or not a woman can preach and proclaim the Gospel today. Women's voices are *still* muted or distorted. The church continues to struggle with issues around women's leadership. And yet, it was Jesus himself who commissioned a woman, Mary of Magdala, with the ultimate Good News of Easter. Scholars today agree on her true identity . . . woman healed, ardent disciple, leader in the early church, apostle to the apostles, first proclaimer of the Easter message. If the tradition of Mary, woman shamed, has done its damage, cannot her true identity, woman as faithful disciple and powerful preacher, help heal the church?

## SOME RESOURCES

Fiorenza, Elisabeth Schüssler. "The Gospel of Mary Magdalene." In *Searching the Scriptures, Vol. 2,* edited by Elisabeth Schüssler Fiorenza, pp. 601-634. New York: The Crossroad Publishing Company, 1994.

Haskins, Susan. *Mary Magdalen, Myth and Metaphor.* New York: Harcourt-Brace, 1993.

O'Day, Gail R. "John." In *Women's Bible Commentary, Expanded Edition,* edited by Carol A. Newsom and Sharon H. Ringe, pp. 381-393. Louisville, KY: Westminster John Knox Press, 1998.

Ricci, Carla. *Mary Magdalene and Many Others.* Minneapolis: Fortress Press, 1994.

Schneiders, Sandra M. *Written That You May Believe: Encountering Jesus in the Fourth Gospel.* A Herder & Herder Book. New York: The Crossroad Publishing Company, 1999.

Thompson, Mary R., S.S.M.N. *Mary of Magdala: Apostle and Leader.* New York and Mahwah, NJ: Paulist Press, 1995.

Weems, Renita. *Just a Sister Away: A Womanist Vision of Women's Relationships in the Bible.* San Diego, CA: LuraMedia, 1988.

## NOTES

1. Mary R. Thompson, S.S.M.N., *Mary of Magdala: Apostle and Leader* (New York and Mahwah, NJ: Paulist Press, 1995), pp. 11-12; hereafter referred to as Thompson.

2. Renita J. Weems, *Just a Sister Away: A Womanist Vision of Women's Relationships in the Bible* (San Diego, CA: LuraMedia, 1988), p. 90.

3. This is not part of the original ending of Mark but is found in the longer ending, 16:9-11. Luke preserves an alternative tradition that Peter is the first to encounter the risen Jesus, Luke 24:34, one that has developed primacy in the West.

4. In John's theology authentic witness is always based on what one has seen and heard. The disciples in John 20:25 bear such witness to Thomas, who was absent on Easter night.

5. In her book, *Written That You May Believe* (New York: The Crossroad Publishing Company, 1999), Sandra M. Schneiders unpacks the meaning of the people to whom Jesus sends Mary in John 20:17. For the first time in this Gospel, John uses the Greek word *adelphoi*, which means siblings (literally brethren, but intended to include women); the disciples are the new family of Jesus ("my Father and your Father, my God and your God"). For John, Jesus enters his glory on the cross; but "resurrection is the communication to Jesus' disciples of his paschal glory through his return to them in the Spirit" (p. 190). Thus, Jesus lives forever with God in glory *and* within the community of disciples, who are the new temple and the new Israel (p. 200).

6. "The Gospel of Mary Magdalene," as found in *Searching the Scriptures, Vol. 2*, edited by Elisabeth Schüssler Fiorenza (New York: The Crossroad Publishing Company, 1994), pp. 610-617.

7. Marjorie Malvern, *Venus in Sackcloth* (Carbondale: South Illinois University Press, 1975), p. 69, as found in Thompson, p. 2.

8. The most famous source of information about these legends, which made Mary of Magdala into a fictionalized and highly dramatic person, is *The Golden Legend* of Jacobus de Voraigne, who died in 1298.

9. Carla Ricci, *Mary Magdalene and Many Others* (Minneapolis: Fortress Press, 1994), pp. 39-40, quoting from p. 13 of the book edited by E. Duperray and C. Loury, p. 13; hereafter referred to as Ricci.

10. Ricci, p. 35, who quotes from Fernand Prat, *Jesus Christ*, p. 504, who quotes from an article by J. Sickenberger.

GLORIA ULTERINO is an active preacher, storyteller, and leader of *"Women of the Well,"* a storytelling group in Rochester, N.Y. She has led the services in this book in parishes and retreat settings, and with various groups since 1998. She holds master's degrees in Divinity, Theology, and Recent American History and is the author of numerous articles on pastoral ministry.